DINGHY SAILING

Ken Duxbury

Ken Duxbury started sailing in 1942 as an Officer in the Royal Navy and has been afloat for much of the time since. On leaving the service he bought his own fourteen-ton cutter and spent five idyllic years living aboard while exploring the coasts of the West Country and South Wales. Eventually, he started a school of sailing on a North Cornish estuary, and eleven years as Principal of this highly successful school has given him a deep insight into the problems besetting the amateur sailor.

Dinghy Sailing

KEN DUXBURY

SPHERE BOOKS LIMITED
30/32 Gray's Inn Road, London, WC1X 8JL

First published in Great Britain in 1970
by Pelham Books Ltd.
© Ken Duxbury 1970
First Sphere Books edition 1972

Printed in Great Britain by
Hazell Watson & Viney Ltd,
Aylesbury, Bucks

Contents

Acknowledgements

My thanks are due to many who responded to my en-
quiries when compiling this book. Most particularly to Duncan
Andrews for condensing much hot air in the weather section.
To G. W. Lennon of the Institute of Coastal Oceanography
and Tides, Birkenhead, for valuable comments on tide gener-
ating forces. To John Morwood, Editor of the Amateur Yacht
Research Society publications and to T. Tanner, senior lecturer
at the Department of Aeronautics and Astronautics, the Univer-
sity, Southampton, for guidance on the involved subject of airflow round sails. To Bramber Engineering Co. Ltd. of Willand
in Devon and the Automobile Association legal services branch
for help in the 'Laws on trailing dinghies'. To John Bray for
late hours spent photographing the knots.

Lastly, to my wife, who now knows exactly how many hours
it takes to type some 200,000 words and then sift, shape,
remould and condense them down to a mere 55,000. Without
her the book would not have been written.

List of Illustrations

Photographs

appearing between pages 88 and 89

Drawings

Preface

Umpteen thousand tons of majestic grey steel loomed ahead. One of His Majesty's capital ships was nosing her way gently through the harbour. From my almost motionless dinghy I watched in awe as she swung in a wide arc which was to bring her even closer to my fragile boat . . . then stared fascinated as a thin necklace of cable came into view, looping down to a massive barrel-shaped buoy ahead of her.

She was PUSHING THE BUOY!

In silent, totally impossible fact she was pushing the buoy like a great ram on the end of that ridiculous cable. Hypnotised into icy inaction I watched as the whole immense nightmare swung head-on a few yards away and bore down on me.

What would you have done? I did. Both arms locked round the bottom links of that cable as a sickening crunch triggered off every survival instinct. Battleships don't bounce. The dinghy did an inverted gavotte athwart the buoy and slid in a capsized tangle of sail, rope, wire and floating equipment along the entire rivet-studded length of the ship's side. Taut rigging twanged on steel plate: runnels were gouged along lovingly varnished planking. I heaved myself on top of the buoy and trembled.

Twenty minutes later, suffering the total ignominy of being made to stand on a spread newspaper in the scrubbed cockpit of a Naval launch (I was plastered in His Majesty's axle grease from the cable), I was carted ashore to face the music . . . and that is another story.

Such is one of my earliest memories of sailing. I was very

9

green then and learning the hard way what tidal streams can do. Of course that ship wasn't moving: she was firmly moored to the bed of the harbour. It was my world of water—carrying me with it—which had been moving past her at some four knots.

I did!

As Einstein might have pointed out: it's all a matter of relativity. Indeed uncle Einstein has been an active and valued member of my crew ever since, for almost everything you do in a sailing dinghy is related to wind, water, and the shore. A beginner in a boat can rely on one certainty . . . not one of those three will ever be quite where you expect it to be!

I learned much that day and have been learning for some twenty-five years since in dinghies, yachts and Her Majesty's ships around the coast of England, and far afield as the United States and Burma. I'm still learning.

This is part of the fascination of sailing: the sport is always presenting problems the nature of which you've not had to face before ... and it's fun. Given a heathen sense of humour such

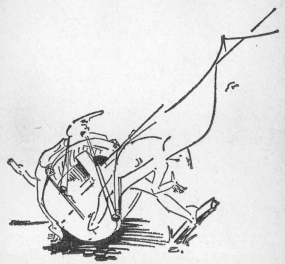

More improbable messes than
a troupe of clowns—

as mine it's more than fun—it can be very funny. I still chuckle when watching the activity on a beach where dinghies are frolicking. Some people get into more improbable messes mishandling one hundred and thirty square feet of frisky terylene than a troupe of clowns. What's more—it seems to do something to their adrenalin glands. They can become fiends. Lovebirds shriek at each other. Sedate gentlemen FOAM! This is no exaggeration: go watch them on any blustery day and you'll go home glowing.

This book is intended for the complete beginner who is thinking of taking up dinghy sailing. You cannot do better than start in a small dinghy because the boat's responses to the wind, and your own reactions to those responses, must be like greased lightning. When you move on to bigger boats—something with a lid on for the whole family to enjoy—you will really get the best possible performance out of them, and it will be child's play.

At the risk of being thought presumptious I can honestly say there is no emotion, be it elation, apprehension, or plain gibbering fear which I have not experienced myself and shared intimately thousands of times with pupils during the past twelve years while Principal of a sailing school.

I'm only half mad now. One cannot say more for the sport! Come on—let's go and drown on paper.

K.D.

1

The Theory of it

THE WIND AND YOU

In order to sail a boat it is not essential to understand exactly how and why the boat responds to the wind. But a good understanding does make the sport more interesting, and for those who are starting from scratch it really helps when you first shove off with the tiller in your unco-ordinated hand to know what you are trying to do. If you do it all in your mind's eye first your reactions will become automatic more quickly and you might even be saved a cold dip, though I doubt it.

Everything . . . just everything you do when sailing a dinghy is related to the wind. Wind is the power you are tapping and it may either propel you, retard you, or capsize you depending on how you use it. A practised helmsman is acutely sensitive to the wind direction and strength relative to his body and the boat. In fact a really good helmsman and crew will consider the boat almost as an extension of his senses. It may be unconsciously so, but only because he has had enough practical experience for his reactions to have become fully automatic. This leaves his conscious attention free to think of wider aims, such as winning a race.

But you cannot skip the early learning processes. One must experience and think about them before one's reactions can speed up. It's in the learning that the real fun and excitement lies . . . after all there's no thrill in the act of walking now, is there? But that was a great day when first your baby head wobbled unsteadily some three feet above the carpet. A whale of a lot of muscular reactions were being 'fed in' then. They

13

are still there, though you'd have to dig deep to find them and if you did make yourself become conscious of them today you'd probably break your neck!

So think about the wind; I hope it will play a great part in your life henceforth. In fact, let's carry out a simple experiment. Tie a piece of light thread to one end of a cane and go out to the clearest piece of ground you can find, preferably with a friend. Choose a day when there is some wind and stick the free end of the cane into the ground so that the thread at the top blows out to give a true wind direction. Stand clear, shut your eyes, and turn round three or four times as quickly as you can with your eyes tight shut. Pick yourself up, and still keeping your eyes shut point directly up wind: that is to say try to point to exactly where (in your opinion) the wind is coming from. Now open your eyes and check your estimate with the blown thread. The friend will stop you cheating and explain things to the police.

You may be accurate or you may not, but in my experience the pupil who can point unerringly straight up wind after a few of these simple tests is off to a flying start where dinghy sailing is concerned.

Now analyse how you decided in your temporarily dark and disorientated world from exactly which point the wind was blowing. You used two sensations: touch and temperature. You felt the wind blowing on your skin, and your skin felt slightly cooler on that half of your face. It's surprising what accuracy can be obtained from these two combined sensations: one learns to strike a sort of mean or average direction indicated by them, and after a while your assessment may be 'spot on'. You will find yourself pointing straight into the eye of the wind, which is a sailor's term meaning straight up wind from you. You have in fact just established the datum line to which all your future fun in boats is related—that datum line is simply the line down which the wind is blowing at you. In a nutshell, you've discovered where the wind is!

HOW DOES A BOAT USE THE WIND?

I propose first to outline briefly what can and what cannot be done when sailing a dinghy, then to study in some detail the sails and each of the points we have covered. I shall assume that we all know what is meant by the hull, mast and sail of a boat.

Anybody can see that a boat will blow down wind. A boat with no sails at all will do that. Pressure of the wind on her hull and all the paraphernalia of the rigging—wires and ropes—and even the chaps sitting in her and the mast itself will be quite sufficient to blow the boat along. There won't be much you can do about the direction either: down wind it will be. Hoist a sail and, provided the sail is used properly, the boat will blow down wind a lot faster but you will now be able to make a fairly wide choice with regard to direction of movement. If at the same time you also lower a deep metal or wooden blade down into the water beneath and in line with the hull (called a centreplate or centreboard) you will really begin to feel that so far as control of direction is concerned you are no longer at the mercy of the wind. In fact you can even choose to sail up into the wind if you wish, which is a bit odd when you think about it.

But it is true. Imagine yourself to be in a sailing dinghy halfway up the crease which separates these two pages. Now imagine the wind to be blowing down that crease from the top: in other words if you look into the eye of the wind you will be looking up the crease. In an efficient sailing dinghy you will now have the choice of directing your movement either straight down the crease towards the bottom of the page—this is called 'running before the wind'—or you may sail across the page in line with the print—called 'sailing on a reach'—or even up toward the wind at an angle of roughly 45 degrees either side that crease which is the wind line. This last is called 'sailing close hauled'.

These three terms, 'running before the wind', 'sailing on a reach', and 'sailing close hauled' are known as points of sailing and there are one or two more points of sailing in between these basic three but we will not bother about them yet.

Look at Figure 1 to make sure these three points of sailing are quite clear.

That angle of roughly 45 degrees either side the wind represents the minimum effective angle that your boat can be turned into the wind and still remain sailing. It is no use trying to sail within that angle, because your sails will simply commence to

15

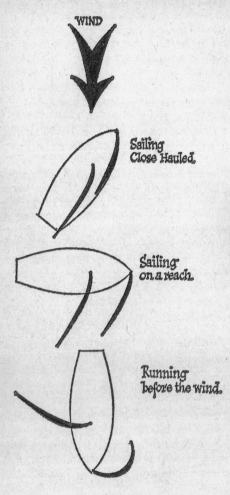

WIND

Sailing
Close Hauled

Sailing
on a reach

Running
before the wind

Figure 1

Points of Sailing

flap and if you try to sail straight into the eye of the wind you will rapidly stop and start going backwards.

So you see, wherever you are if you stand facing up into the eye of the wind and hold your arms out at full length pointing 45 degrees either side of the wind line, you will know that you can sail anywhere right round the circle of 360 degrees except within that 90 degrees sector which your arms are dividing off. If you wish to sail up to a destination within that 90 degrees sector you will have to sail close hauled first in the direction one arm is pointing, then turn your boat through the eye of the wind to bring it on to the opposite side and then sail at 90 degrees to your first direction. You will have to repeat this manoeuvre as often as necessary working your way in a series of zig-zags up into the wind. This is called 'beating to windward'.

For me, sailing close hauled is by far the most interesting and satisfying point of sailing because of the feeling that one is getting something for nothing ... after all the wind itself is being used to blow the boat against the wind, and it's all a bit odd!

In point of fact it is not quite like that.

It is nearer the truth to say that when sailing close hauled the deflection of the wind by your sails causes the boat to be squeezed between wind and water which results in it being moved in a forward direction. The fact that it moves forward is due simply to the aerofoil shape of the sail and the manner in which it is presented to the wind line, coupled with the shape of the boat's hull and centreboard.

The mainsail is the large sail and do you see it is curved from front to back so that if you looked straight down from the top of the mast it would appear like this:

Figure 2

Curvature of Mainsail

This curvature, or aerofoil shape, does surprising things to the wind which passes either side of it. If it were just flat it would not work at all well, and to understand why this curvature makes such a difference we cannot do better than look at the wing of an aeroplane which is a splendid example of an aerofoil.

Next time you're up at 40,000 feet look at the shape of that wing, particularly in its section (i.e. chopped clean through from front to back edge). You will see it has a markedly curved upper side and a flattish lower side. If it were not so you would have to reach for a parachute for it is only because the wings are aerofoil in section that the plane and you stay up there.

A boat's sail is very like a plane's wing stuck up on end though, alas, it is not nearly so efficient because a sail is made of thin cloth whereas a wing is made of rigid alloy and therefore has a lower edge which remains flat. Just as a wing supplies 'lift'—a vertical force acting upwards—so a sail supplies 'thrust' —a force acting sideways. But as in the case of a wing, it is vital that the sail also is presented to the wind at the correct angle. If it is, the thrust resulting from its aerofoil shape will lie in a direction slightly forward of a right-angle to the overall plane of the sail. When this thrust is related to the fore-and-aft line of the boat beneath the sail it can only result in the boat moving forward.

Now think about the boat: the hull cannot easily move sideways—you dropped that centreboard down specifically to stop it doing so, and for no other reason. (Try drawing a hot knife through butter and you will see what I mean.) But the centreboard and the hull will allow forward or backward movement. The thrust from the sail, even when sailing close hauled, is slightly forwards—so forwards the boat has to go, squeezed in a remarkable way between wind and water.

There is one sentence in the paragraph above which should be emphasized. I wrote: 'it is vital that the sail is PRESENTED TO THE WIND AT THE CORRECT ANGLE'.

This angle is the all important factor. It makes the difference between winning and losing races, between feeling that your boat is really a live thing, or just not feeling anything except being blown about in a random way.

So now, before we think in detail about this angle the sail makes to the wind, and the resultant thrust generated by its aerofoil shape, it will be useful to take a good look at the boat, sails and ropes, learning the names of the important parts. Figure 3 will help.

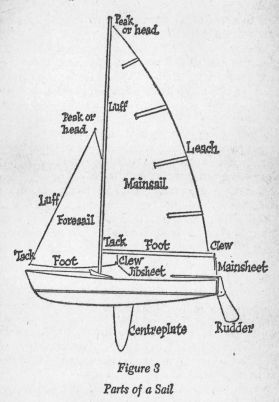

Figure 3

Parts of a Sail

THE PARTS OF A SAIL

Most modern dinghies are rigged with Bermudan sails, and the word 'rigged' is a sailor's term which means 'equipped and ready to operate'. The name Bermudan indicates that the shape of the sail is roughly a triangle as opposed to a square or trapezium. The name has (so far as I know) nothing whatever to do with Bermuda and I've never heard a satisfactory explanation as to why this name should have been adopted. In earlier days the square shape and trapezium were commonly used, but from experience it was found that the triangular sail —particularly a tall triangle where the front edge was much longer than the bottom edge—was far more efficient when sailing close hauled or on a reach.

This is true of the single Bermudan sail, but if two Bermudan sails are used and set in a critical position relative to each other, the thrust of the whole assembly is slightly increased. Sometimes boats are rigged with a single sail only and are then often referred to as being 'una rigged'. Boats with two sails (the larger one on the mast and the smaller one forward of the mast) are referred to as being 'sloop rigged'. A sloop with two triangular sails will therefore be called a Bermudan sloop.

The boat in Figure 3 is rigged as a Bermudan sloop. Learn off by heart the names of all three edges of the sails and also their corners. I would only remark here that the top corner of the sail is often referred to as the Head, as well as being called the Peak. Strictly, Peak is more correct for reasons which will become apparent when we come to consider the evolution of sail shapes throughout the ages. But by common usage Head is gradually superseding the correct name. I learned the names of the three corners 'Tack' 'Clew' and 'Peak' by associating their first letters 'TCP' with the well known antiseptic. It helped trigger off the rest of the names!

You will see that the large sail is called the mainsail and the smaller one forward of the mast is the foresail. Often there are two sizes of foresail available with a dinghy, particularly with racing dinghies, in which case the smaller one is called a Jib and the larger a Genoa. The illustration in Figure 3 is a Wayfarer dinghy and the foresail shown is a Genoa, of course the Jib and Genoa cannot be hoisted at the same time. It's a matter of choice which foresail you 'set' and this choice will depend on the strength of wind and your own confidence. The Genoa will give more thrust being larger, but it is not an unmixed blessing on that account because it does tend to be slightly less efficient when sailing close hauled unless it is cut specifically

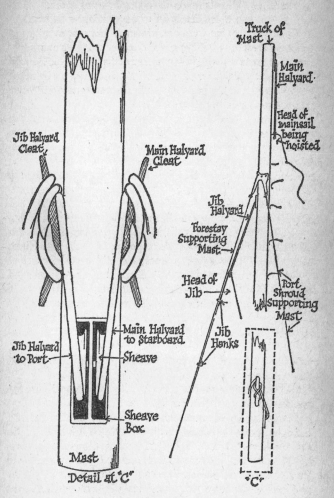

Figure 4

Position of Halyards on mast

for beating by the sailmaker. So if you are trying really hard to beat to windward the fact that you are using a Genoa may result in your having to sail at a slightly greater angle to the wind which means that you will have to travel farther (even though it may be a little faster). On a reach however, the Genoa is a real advantage.

Both mainsail and foresail are hoisted by means of a rope or wire (or sometimes a combination of both) called a halyard. One therefore has a main halyard and a Jib halyard, the latter for hoisting either Jib or Genoa. In most metal masts these run down inside the mast emerging at top and bottom as shown in Figure 4.

Once hoisted, the leach of both sails will start flogging madly in a brisk wind, rather like a flag on a mast. So in order to harness the potential power of the wind one must control the angle the sail makes with the wind line and this is done by means of a rope attached to the clew of the sail called a 'sheet'.

Remember that a sheet is the rope, and NOT the sail. Never refer to this rope as a rope: not even a sheetrope, otherwise any sailor within hearing distance will collapse! I know no valid reason why it should not be called a rope, but DON'T!

So one has a mainsheet which controls the mainsail, and a jibsheet which controls the Jib or Genoa, and the degree to which either or both of these sails should be 'trimmed' in or out relative to the hull of the boat entirely depends on the angle that the fore-and-aft line of the hull is making with the wind line.

I'll bet that's flummoxed you! Read it again: it means exactly what it says, and to make it sink in look at Figure 5.

Pay particular attention to the angle the wind is making with the fore-and-aft line of the hull. Watch the angle of the sail relative to this fore-and-aft line of the hull as the boat turns more across the wind from a close hauled position on to the reach. Do you see how the sail itself is being allowed to maintain exactly the same angle to the wind, even though the boat's hull is turning more across the wind?

Can you see why? Suppose the sail was not eased out as the boat turned across the wind. It's fairly obvious that the force of the wind would simply bring more pressure sideways on the

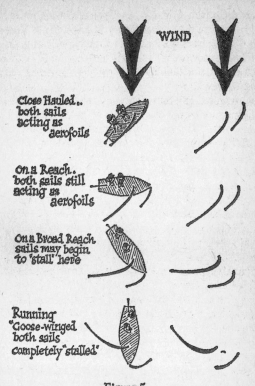

Figure 5

*Angle of Hull and Sails to Wind Line
on Different Points of Sailing*

sail. The mast would lever the boat violently over because the centreboard is preventing the hull skidding sideways, and if the wind was strong enough a capsize might result.

By easing the sheet and thus allowing the sail to maintain the same angle with the wind as when the boat was close hauled, the boat will immediately start to move forward. This is not due entirely to pressure on the sail—it's a bit more subtle than that, and this is where we can begin to study the action of an aerofoil. First, however, we must clearly understand two more nautical terms, namely 'windward' and 'leeward'. Everything on the same side of an object as the eye of the wind is said to be to windward (or on the windward side) of that object. Everything on the opposite side of the object to the eye of the wind is said to be to leeward (or on the leeward side) of that object. In Figure 6 the buoy is to windward of the boat, and the seagull is to leeward of the boat.

Figure 6

Windward and Leeward

Look again at the shape and position of the sail in Figure 5. The sail is curved at the front edge (luff) and flattens out towards the trailing edge (leach).

THE AEROFOIL

When a sail is trimmed correctly (as in the top examples of Figure 5) to the wind the latter will flow on to the luff of the sail at a very small angle of incidence. The plane of the sailcloth at the luff will be very nearly in line with the wind line. As the curvature of the cloth sweeps round from the straight line however, the wind will also be swept round by deflection and temporarily take up a new direction parallel to the sail-cloth. At the leach therefore it will flow off the sail roughly in the same plane as the leach. In being deflected like this, the wind is forced to slow up a little which results in a slight pressure being built up on the windward side of the sail. On the leeward side however, things are very different. In order to travel round the greater distance on the leeward curve the wind has to speed up a bit and in so doing presents what can best be described as a partial vacuum. You may actually see this happening if you care to drag a teaspoon sideways (along its section) through a bowl of salt. The spoon is a crude aerofoil and you can see the salt building up into a hump on the concave (windward) side where a slight pressure is being formed. On the convex (leeward) side however there will be a hollow where the grains have had to stretch in space so as to get round the curve fast enough.

This twofold action of pressure on the windward side of a sail and partial vacuum on the leeward side results in myriads of small forces acting all over the sail, and from detailed experiments in wind tunnels using scale model sails and smoke to make the wind visible, these forces have been pictorially plotted by drawing small arrows to indicate the directions of force. The length of the arrows indicates the strength of the force (see Figure 7). It is important to realise in this diagram that the force represented by any one of the arrows is always acting at right angles to the cloth at that point.

Now consider the relative position of the two aerofoils, jib and main. We have seen that at the leach of a correctly trimmed sail the airflow, particularly at the lower area of the sail, has been deflected from its original course. The mainsail, since its foot is attached to the boom, is presenting a slightly greater angle to the wind line at its lower area since the sail twists slightly as it goes up towards the peak. So if the luff at the peak of the sail is trimmed to a correct angle of incidence, it is likely that the luff near the lower area of the sail will be at too great an angle with the wind and this results in what is called 'stalling' of the sail. The wind at this lower part of the luff will not flow cleanly along the plane of the sailcloth if this happens; instead the airflow breaks down and turbulence sets in which destroys the thrust forces in the area. To a certain extent this is catered for by the sailmaker putting a greater 'fullness' into the sail at the lower part.

But this moment of stalling at the lower part of the luff of the main may also be delayed due to the jib deflecting the airflow into a more acceptable angle of attack. The airflow coming off

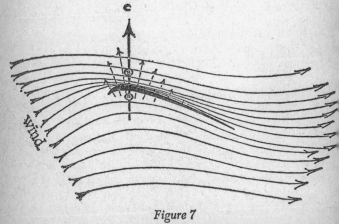

Figure 7

How a sail works

A sail is a primitive aerofoil in so far as the main airstream is deflected from its course by the sail's curvature. In being deflected the air to windward of the sail slows up and therefore exerts a pressure at 'A'. Conversely the wind passing round the leeward side of the sail has to speed up, which results in a slight lessening of pressure at 'B'. The lines of 'push' and 'pull' act at right angles to the surface of the sail and if you consider the combined effect of them all it would thrust in the direction of arrow 'C'. Relate this direction to the fore-and-aft line of the boat and you will see why the boat has to move forward. It cannot move sideways because of the centreboard.

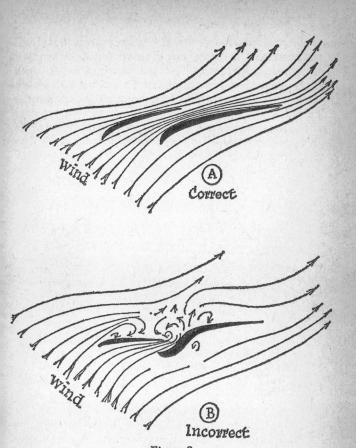

Figure 8

Action of jib on main

(A) Correct.   (B) Incorrect

The trim of the jib may either augment or destroy the thrust of the main. In diagram 'B' above the jib is sheeted in far too hard. This is completely destroying the drive of the main because the aerofoil shape is ruined. In diagram 'A' the jib is correctly sheeted, and while it is acting as an aerofoil in its own right it is also augmenting the aerofoil thrust of the main by the leach area of the jib has already been deflected from its original course, and more so at the lower part of the jib than the upper. Apart from acting as aerofoils in their own right therefore, in this relationship of jib and main the jib can in fact augment the thrust of the main by increasing the efficiency of the luff in the lower part and you will now understand how critical is the amount that the jib must be sheeted home in relation to the mainsail, most particularly when sailing close hauled. Sheet the jib in too hard and you will not only destroy its own aerofoil action but you will also completely disrupt the airflow at the luff of the main by deflecting it round actually on to the leeward surface of the luff instead of along it.

This is what I meant when I said that a really good helmsman and crew will treat the boat and sails as an extension of their senses: you can actually feel when you are mucking it all up. When sailing close hauled with a well designed sailplan, if the jib is correctly trimmed to act as an aerofoil in its own right, it will also be in the correct position to effect an augmentation of the mainsail's thrust. (See Figure 8.)

---

deflecting the airflow to a more acceptable angle of incidence to the latter at the lower part of the luff, thus delaying the moment of stalling.

It is sometimes thought that by the squeezing (and therefore speeding up) of the airflow between the leach of the jib and the luff of the main a 'venturi' action results—i.e. the creation of a partial vacuum between the two sails. In my opinion this is suspect. If a venturi action could possibly be so caused between the two sails it is probable that the leach of the jib would merely be sucked in toward the luff of the main. Or alternatively, if the minimum pressure point were just aft of the jib leach it would tend to move the maximum thrust line (centre of effort) of the mainsail too far aft to be really effective as a forward thrust component when sailing close hauled.

The whole situation with an airflow acting on two aerofoils in close proximity is incredibly complex and the overall effect depends on sail shape, proximity, trim and speed of airflow among other things.

Look again at Figure 7. You will have noticed that the lines of greater force (length) are toward the luff of the sail, and at this point (since they act at right angles to the surface of the cloth) they tend to drive the boat in a forward direction. All the myriad of small arrows of force distributed over the surface of the sail may, for convenience, be resolved into just one large force which will be the combined effect of all the forces. If drawn in this will be found to lie roughly in a direction and with a strength shown in Figure 9. The point on the sail through which this force acts is referred to as the 'Centre of Effort' of the sail.

The boat in Figure 9 is sailing close hauled. Do you now clearly understand why she is squeezed in a forward direction even though she is sailing into the wind? It is simply because the arrow of force at the centre of effort of the sails is angled well forward (about 20 degrees) of a right angle drawn from

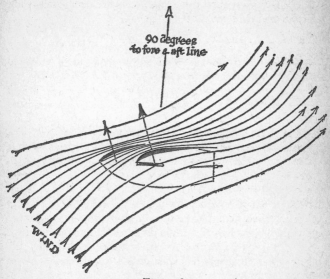

Figure 9

Resultant thrust and centre-of-effort of a sail

the fore-and-aft line of the hull. If the boat were allowed to skid sideways to leeward of course it would do so and the boat would not move forward. But you remember the hull and centreboard are shaped specially to prevent this skidding—it is called 'making leeway'. So the boat is squeezed between the pressure of water to leeward of the hull and centreboard, and the combined force on the sails consisting of pressure to windward and partial suction to leeward.

What's more—it works!

Now do a simple experiment. Imagine the boat to be sailing close hauled with both sails sheeted correctly to get maximum aerofoil action. Now turn the boat slowly round off the wind towards the reach and ease the sheets just enough (not too much or the luff will start 'lifting') so as to maintain the delicate balance of power and continue turning the boat until one is running before the wind.

At some point you will have found that you could no longer continue to ease out those sheets in order that the sails could maintain their correct aerofoil angle to the wind. The sheets were just not long enough, and in any case beyond a certain point the wires that hold up the mast got in the way. So the sails began to present an incorrect angle to the wind—they had reached their moment of stalling, as illustrated in Figure 5. As the boat turned still farther down wind both sails are completely stalled. All aerofoil action has now broken down and the sails are merely acting as a rather badly designed parachute. A large part of the available power of the wind has now been lost and this accounts for a mystery which baffles many sailors who do not fully understand how a sail uses the wind: running before the wind is much slower than sailing on a reach or close hauled. It sounds unreasonable, but you should now understand why!

It will be well at this point to relate the different points of sailing to the different positions of the centreboard for it should now be evident that when beating to windward the plate should be fully down and should be progressively raised the more the boat comes off the wind until when running dead before the wind no plate is required. We will discuss this in more detail in Chapter Two.

THE TACK AND THE GYBE

Now that we understand the principle of why a well designed sail works and how it is used to harness power in a given direction relative to the plane of the sail and the hull of the boat, we can consider in detail the way in which a boat can 'beat to windward' in order to sail up to a destination straight in the eye of the wind.

Look at Figure 10. The boat starts at the bottom of the page sailing close hauled with the wind blowing on to the left side of sails and hull. In sailor's language this is the Port side, and it is useful to understand a subtle difference between 'Port' and 'Left'. The truth is, merely to refer to it as the left side is not accurate enough for a sailor: face the stern of the boat and the left side is no longer the Port side, is it! So a sailor when he says 'Port' always means the left side of the boat WHEN FACING THE BOW.

At the bottom of the page therefore the boat starts with the wind blowing on the Port side and she is then said to be sailing close hauled on the port tack. When used in this sense the word tack simply means 'side'.

In order not to sail over the edge of the page the boat has to turn by bringing the bow up into the eye of the wind, then continue turning until the wind blows on the right hand side of sails and hull. She is now sailing close hauled on the Starboard tack, and will have turned through about 90 degrees from her original course. The word 'Starboard' means right hand side when looking towards the bow.

We have seen how the word 'tack' may be used in two senses, both incidentally as nouns. You may be sailing on Port or Starboard tack, or you may be referring to the tack of the sail which is the forward bottom corner. There is yet a third meaning: the word may also be used as a verb: 'to tack'.

The verb 'to tack' simply means the act of turning the boat up through the eye of the wind in order to bring the wind on to the opposite side. She tacks twice in Figure 10—at each of the points where she turns.

So that there can be no doubt as to the use of these words, I'm going to describe, detail by detail, what the boat does in Figure 10.

Starting at the foot of the page she sails close hauled on the Port tack. Having arrived at the right hand edge of the page she tacks by bringing her bow up and round through the eye of the wind and continues turning until the sails present that critical angle to the wind line which results in her sailing close hauled on the Starboard tack until she has to tack again due to the crease. She now turns the other way and executes a tack so that she once more sails close hauled on the Port tack. Each time she tacks she swings through roughly 90 degrees—about 45 degrees either side of the wind—and by continuing to zig-zag in this fashion she works her way up into the eye of the wind to the destination 'X'. This zig-zag course is called 'beating to windward'. So if you are beating to windward you are automatically sailing close hauled on alternate tacks.

Now imagine yourself in the boat sailing close hauled on the Port tack. As you arrive at the edge of the page you steer the boat round through 90 degrees to bring her on to the Starboard tack. I want you to imagine what happens to the sails as you do this.

As soon as you begin steering the boat more towards the eye of the wind, in the very first stage of the turn, you will be bringing the luff of both sails immediately in line with the wind line. You will see this because the luffs will commence to 'lift' and shake, since they are no longer being pressed at one side by the wind. As the boat swings more toward the wind, so progressively more and more of the sails will shake until—when the boat's fore-and-aft line is pointing dead into the eye of the wind—every part of the sail from luff to leach will be shaking, and no thrust at all will be derived from the wind, except a pressure directly backwards!

It is important that you do not remain at this critical stage of the turn otherwise the forward momentum of the boat will soon be lost and then (unless you are quite experienced) you will also have lost control of the boat. If you think of it, it's only because you are moving through the water that your rudder acts at all in a sailing boat. If you lose your forward momentum when turning you will get 'in irons'—a descriptive term to indicate that you have lost control through bad management. Unless you are careful the boat will start moving backwards when 'in irons'.

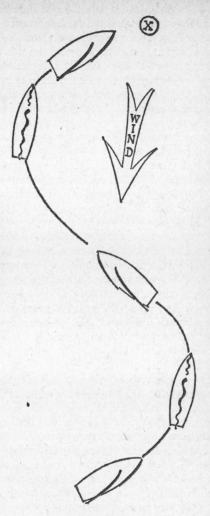

Figure 10
Beating to windward

So far we have turned through about 45 degrees of the full 90 degrees from our original course, and this turning up into the eye of the wind is only the preliminary to the act of tacking. YOU HAVE NOT YET COMMENCED TO TACK. Get this quite clear: changing from one tack to another falls into two distinct parts and you have now completed only the first part, namely turning the boat from your original course up into the eye of the wind. It is called 'luffing up'. You should readily see why it is called 'luffing'—it is the luff of the sails which begin to shake immediately you turn towards the wind.

The remaining half of the turn constitutes the tack. For ease of speaking the total turn of 90 degrees is loosely called 'tacking' but it is necessary to understand that until the bow is straight into the eye of the wind she is 'luffing up' and as such the boat is still technically on the original tack. As soon as the bow has swung through the eye of the wind she is on neither tack, until her mainsail again fills. This is important when interpreting the Collision Regulations for sailing boats, because Starboard tack boats have right of way over Port tack boats and you must be able to define exactly who is on port and who is on Starboard tack without ambiguity.

So much for tacking. Now I want you to consider what may perhaps be thought of as the exact opposite of tacking: the 'Gybe'.

In Figure 11 the boat starts from the top of the page and sails toward the bottom, but in doing so has to negotiate an obstruction in the form of a headland. You will see that when she starts at the top of the page she is running before the wind on the Port tack, since the wind is blowing slightly on to the Port side of the boat. This is called sailing on a 'broad reach'. To miss the headland she has to sail right over to the edge of the page and then alter course to Starboard in order to reach her destination 'Y' at the bottom left hand corner.

As she turns to run dead before the wind, the jib will be blanketed by the mainsail so it is brought out on the Port side of the boat so that the sails are set on opposite sides. This is called 'running goosewinged'. We are still on the Port tack for although in fact the wind is not actually blowing on to either side of the boat, but from straight astern, because the mainsail

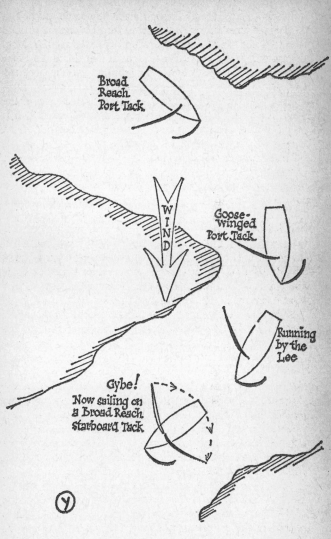

Broad
Reach
Port Tack

WIND

Goose-
winged
Port Tack

Running
by the
Lee

Gybe!
Now sailing on
a Broad Reach
starboard Tack

Y

Figure 11
Gybing

35

is on the Starboard side of the boat she is still deemed to be on Port tack.

As she proceeds to turn still more to Starboard there will come a point where the wind is blowing between the mainsail and the fore-and-aft line of the boat. This is called 'running by the lee', but beware ... do you see what is going to happen?

At some point as she turns, the wind is going to whip round behind that mainsail and slam it across with the full pressure of wind in it. If the wind is strong enough and you are not prepared it can easily knock you overboard with the boom. It may even capsize the boat if you are not already shifting your weight into a counterbalancing position as the boom swings across: and it has to be fast!

This act of allowing—or causing—the mainsail to swing across by passing the eye of the wind across the stern of a boat is called 'Gybing' and it's great fun. In fact it causes more accidental capsizes in sailing dinghies than any other factor.

Do you now understand the essential difference between tacking and gybing? In the former the boat's bow swings up through the eye of the wind and the sails can only shake harmlessly as she turns. In the latter the stern is swung through the eye of the wind and this can only result in a relatively violent change of position for the sail. In both cases one has changed the tack upon which one was sailing—but what a difference in the method of doing it!

It is because of the chance of an accidental gybe that running dead before the wind, even though it is the calmest and slowest point of sailing, is in fact the most tricky. One may very easily be lulled into a false sense of security. One tends to lose the sense of wind direction when running and that's when you may easily gybe accidentally. But it is only the ACCIDENTAL gybe which is tricky: provided you know you are going to gybe all will be well since you will be ready to handle the situation by shift of weight and adjustments of the tiller with which you are steering. Sometimes, of course, the wind is just too strong to handle in which case despite all the correct movements you'll probably end up with a swim. Experience will teach you when that point has been reached.

CAPSIZE AND RECOVERY

Contrary to what might be expected the capsize is generally —in its final stages at any rate—a quite slow and sometimes graceful affair. Certainly this is often the case when capsizing to leeward because as the boat heels more and more, so the sails spill more and more wind until she gently dips her side decks under and scoops the water in. After that it depends on you entirely whether you are up to your neck in water—or sitting high and dry on the upper side of the boat. If you are young and lissom the chances are that as the boat heeled over you will have by sheer instinct kept up on top. If, on the other hand, you are caught unawares and fall down into the water then you may as well stay there and work your way round to the centre-board side of the hull in order to use this as a lever to pull down and right her again.

The golden rule, if you do get pitched into the water, is STAY WITH THE BOAT. This may appear obvious to anyone who has never capsized in a brisk wind, but it is not always as easy as it sounds. The fact is, when the boat is lying on her side with the mast and sails along the surface of the water, she will tend to blow to leeward amazingly fast. If you become detached from her (perhaps in trying to swim around the hull to grab the centreboard) you may well find yourself quite unable to recapture the boat—especially if you are hampered by a lifejacket or personal buoyancy waistcoat.

This is not implying that you should ever fail to wear some form of lifejacket when afloat: I mention it simply to point out that they do hamper even a strong swimmer. So whatever you do, if you find yourself in the water after a capsize, grab a sheet or some other portion of the boat, and take good care that you do not lose contact while endeavouring to right her again.

There is nothing so frustrating as to find oneself bobbing in the water well up to windward of the boat which is fast disappearing down on to a lee shore which may well be rock strewn! In addition of course, when the rescue launch comes to collect the bits, it will be to the boat that they come because this is easily seen. A head bobbing in choppy water is very difficult to pick out (practically impossible if viewed against the sun) and you may have to remain soaked for longer than is comfortable.

The capsize to windward, on the other hand, can be violent and sudden. The sort of thing which causes this is a sudden shift in the wind when you are beating to windward. Your weight, and that of your crew, will be poised well out over the weather side to keep the boat upright. Suddenly the wind shifts, or perhaps dies completely, and you are literally almost projected backwards into the water as the boat flips to windward. A violent accidental gybe can cause much the same sensation. In these circumstances you are almost bound to find yourself in the water unless your reactions are lightning fast. After that the procedure is exactly the same as for any righting of the boat.

Now think about the boat immediately after a capsize. Suddenly she has become an inert and partly immersed object with mast and sails roughly along the surface of the water, and at least half of the total hull area may be up above the surface. Exactly how much of the hull remains out of the water depends entirely on how much buoyancy is either built in or tied in to the boat. Most modern dinghies have an area forward and aft (and often down either side as well) which is made completely watertight—they are called buoyancy tanks—specifically to keep the boat afloat when capsized. Others have inflated bags secured in by stout straps—these are called buoyancy bags—and they are fine provided they really are properly secured to a strong part of the boat. How often have I watched these buoyancy bags popping out of capsized boats and blowing gaily away to leeward while the boat sank down awash, quite unable to support her crew!

Before we consider the method of righting the boat I would like to pass a few comments on the 'pros' and 'cons' of hull buoyancy. Firstly of course, a certain amount of buoyancy is very necessary. It should be sufficient to support helmsmen and crew when sitting on the side of the boat which is capsized, and it should support them for an indefinite period. In the unlikely event of their not being able to right the boat and get her sailing again, they should be able to keep themselves more or less dry and certainly out of the water until help comes, or they drift ashore. But too much buoyancy can be a disadvantage when capsized for the very reason that I mentioned earlier: it is dangerous if a member of the crew accidentally becomes separated from the boat. You see, if the boat is literally floating like a cork on her side, the 'windage' (pressure of wind on the exposed hull) will be so great, and the resistance of the very small area of the immersed hull so small, that she will blow across the surface too fast. Even the sails, mast and rigging trailing in the water will not prevent this, and it can be disconcerting when one is trying to catch her up by swimming!

I want you to imagine a small, lightly constructed dinghy in a capsized state with a really brisk wind blowing. To start with the mast and sails will be flat on the water down to leeward (assuming her to have capsized to leeward). Think what happens if she is left entirely to her own devices. The wind presses on the underside of the buoyant hull, and the sails etc. acting as a drogue in the water soon cause the hull to swing in an arc until the sails are trailing to windward, and the hull with its concave side is catching the wind down to leeward of them. If the wind is not too strong she will continue to drift quite fast to leeward in that fashion. If however the wind is strong enough it will push the hull just sufficiently to raise the top of the mast clear of the water. Immediately this happens the wind gets beneath the sail and flips the whole boat up and over the opposite way. Then the whole procedure commences again; the hull arcs round, catches the wind strongly on the mast side, lifts the top of the mast and flips her over again. The result is that she speeds down wind in a series of 'flips' and I have watched a dinghy do this for about half a mile while her late crew manfully swam ashore. Fortunately they were both wearing buoyancy aids, otherwise it might have been a tragedy: it was at Easter and the water was perishing cold. Neither of them could stand on reaching the shore from sheer exhaustion and numbness!

The opposite extreme of course is where a dinghy has not enough buoyancy in the hull. After capsizing there will be little hope (and not much point) in righting her since she will be floating just awash with no chance of sailing again until she has been grounded and bailed out on a falling tide. What is more she will be useless for keeping her crew dry, but this does not imply that they should leave the boat. Better to have something to hold on to which is just floating than nothing at all! Negative buoyancy, where there are no built-in or tied-in buoyancy bags, coupled perhaps with a heavy metal centreplate can of course result in complete sinking. Some of the older classes were prone to this and the only thing to be said in their favour was the fact that generally they were very difficult indeed to capsize. Once they were over however—that was it! You were on your own in the water and measuring the yards to shore.

Now think about righting the modern dinghy after she has capsized. You will have realised that when the boat is lying on her side the centreboard sticking out from the hull makes a very handy lever. If you're in the water anyway you will have to simply reach up and gently pull down on the centreboard, and if you have a crew with you also in the water get him to hold on to the stem of the boat by the forestay at deck level. You will be astonished how easy it is to lever most dinghies upright and provided your crew securely holds on to the bow she will soon swing head to wind. Then you pull yourself aboard OVER THE STERN and start bailing with a large plastic bucket—this should always form part of a boat's equipment unless she has a great deal of buoyancy in the hull which makes it virtually unnecessary to bail by hand. Do not try to climb aboard over the side of the boat otherwise the chances are you'll just capsize her again over on top of you. Remember she will be very unstable with all the water in the cockpit.

It used to be the practice to lower sails before attempting to right a boat, but in most modern dinghies this is no longer necessary for they will take so little water in the cockpit that you might just as well get her sailing immediately.

Of course, thinking of it in theory and doing it in practice are very different, but if you do this in your mind's eye a few times it will help enormously when the real thing happens. Things often go wrong: you think you have the boat upright and are just climbing aboard when the whole blessed paraphernalia capsizes again and in cold water you don't have to go through this many times before you begin to tire. This is when an element of danger creeps in. The great thing is to keep your head and HOLD ON TO THE BOAT. If you find you just cannot get her to remain upright long enough for you to get aboard, then you must lower the sails while she is lying on her side, and right her again. You will find she is much easier to handle without the windage up aloft, and even if you cannot manage to climb back into the boat you'll find it a lot easier to maintain your hold on her until you either drift ashore or the rescue boat comes and fishes you out.

A great deal depends on one's fitness. An active and lithe youngster will find no difficulty whatever in levering himself up over the stern into the cockpit of the boat again. An older, less fit man will find it quite impossible. The former will have her bailed out and sailing within minutes: the latter will just have to drift slowly ashore or wait to be picked up but remember: STAY WITH THE BOAT.

Finally, think of the textbook case where the boat has capsized and an agile crew member is sitting on the upper section of the hull, possibly quite dry. The other chap—not so quick in his reactions—is holding on to the boat near the mast, probably half in and half out of the water. The one thing you have to avoid in this situation is to allow him to pull the boat over so that the mast and sails slowly plumb the depths until

— All right down there?

LET GO!

NOW are you satisfied?

(provided the water is deep enough) they are pointing vertically down with the more active member doing his best to maintain his position on the wet and slippery inverted hull! It's quite possible to right the boat again from this turtle position, but it's not nearly as easy and really should never arise if one's wits are about one.

As soon as it is evident that the mast and sails are beginning to sink below the surface it is imperative that the weight of the crew member sitting on top of the boat should go over towards the centreboard which will be sticking out more or less horizontally. Very gently press on the plate near to the hull (remember this plate is only made of plywood and won't stand two fifteen stone men doing a springboard act!). Using the plate as a lever gently ease the mast and sails back up to the surface, and then as they begin to drag free of the water be ready to pull yourself back aboard and start balancing the boat as soon as she is upright otherwise you'll all be in the water frolicking around amongst sails and rigging with the boat capsized again on top of you!

There are ways of getting back aboard as she rights herself, and we'll think about these when we come to do the thing again in practice later. For the time being just read and re-read this theoretical part until you begin to realise what it's all about.

When it makes sense turn the page and we will start the practical side of it all.

2

Putting it into Practice

SAILING CLOTHES

I loathe being cold, and out on the water it is almost certain to be colder than you expect. Even on a hot day it's likely to get chilly sitting half naked while someone sluices you with buckets of water—and it may be like that 'out there'.

Shorts or a swimsuit are best for the bottom half of one's anatomy because you are certain to get wet up to the knees before long, no matter how careful you are during the launching of the boat. Personally I never wear anything on my feet, preferring that they dry off quickly rather than remain squelchy in any form of shoe. But some people's toes are more tender than mine, and if you do choose shoes, some form of plimsoll with a good grip to the sole is best.

A warm jersey on top is advisable. If you don't actually start out wearing this it is best to take it in the boat properly secured, because after a while you may decide to don it. Over this, in windy or wet weather, I wear my oilskin smock, and I prefer the type with attached hood because although I do, in fact, seldom have this up over my head (I find it inhibits my all-round awareness of the presence of other boats, and also interferes with my exact appreciation of the wind conditions), nevertheless in the sudden downpour it saves a lot of water trickling down one's back and chest! The normal buoyant waistcoat goes over the top of this, if that is the type of personal buoyancy one is wearing. A soft towel wrapped round the neck is a good thing: it soaks up any drops that try to creep down.

The whole object of sailing clothing is twofold: to keep one dry and warm, and to ensure that one is easily seen. It is not from any aesthetic consideration that these lifejackets and smocks are brilliant orange or yellow in colour: it is so that one is easily visible in the water. For this reason I always advise against the dark and light blue smocks, for although they are certainly more versatile in their use—you can play golf or do the shopping in them without feeling quite so self-conscious—they aren't a bit of use when you are hoping to be noticed while blowing out to sea off a weather shore!

THE BOAT

Figure 12 shows a typical modern family sailing dinghy. The boat shown is a Wayfarer class dinghy designed by Ian Proctor M.S.I.A., one of the leading British dinghy designers. She has proved herself to be an excellent all-rounder for she can be raced, or used for cruising and she has some really amazing

Key to Figure 12

1 Shroud
2 Forestay
3 Mast
4 Jib hank
5 Boom
6 Gooseneck
7 Fairlead
8 Foredeck
9 Washboard
10 Mast pivot bolt
11 Centreboard
12 Centreboard casing
13 Thwart
14 Jib sheetlead
15 Rigging screw, connected to chain-plate
16 Side deck
17 Bottom boards
18 Rubbing strake

19 Tiller extension
20 Tiller
21 After deck
22 After buoyancy hatch
23 Sheethorse with mainsheet lower block
24 Tiller retaining pin
25 Transom
26 Rudder hanging
27 Rudder stock
28 Chine
29 Drain bung
30 Keel
31 Folding rudder blade
32 Mainsheet
33 Jibsheet
34 Kicking strap
35 Mainsheet lower block
36 Jib Tack strop

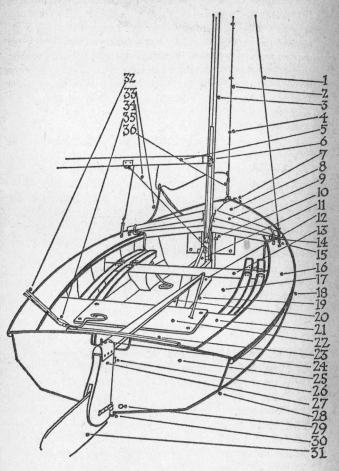

Figure 12
The Wayfarer. A modern family dinghy

47

long distance voyages to her credit across open seas, some of them in gale conditions. It is the Wayfarer that we will be sailing in this Chapter.

First, look at her hull shape.

You will see that her sides drop down from deck level then angle in slightly toward the keel, and then again angle in to join the keel. These angles, which run the length of the hull from near the bow right along aft to the transom, are called 'chines' and since there are two chines this form of hull construction is called double chine. These Wayfarers are constructed of either marine plywood or glassfibre, and in the latter the original form of double chine has been retained.

A boat with only one chine, where the side of the hull drops almost vertically down from deck level and then sharply angles in to join the keel, is referred to as single chine or hard chine construction. A GP 14, one of the most popular two-man dinghies, is hard chine, whereas the Enterprise—perhaps the most popular and prolific of all two-man dinghies—is a double chine boat like this Wayfarer. Figure 13 illustrates these two forms of construction as well as a round bilge hull, such as the Firefly, an exciting little dinghy. These round bilge hulls are generally made of thin laminates of wood laid diagonally to one another and bonded together with coatings of resin glue until they are 'built up' to the required thickness. This is either done in a normal room temperature, in which case the hull would be referred to as 'cold moulded', or they are laid up and then baked in a special large oven which also evacuates the air from inside the mould to ensure an even pressure of the laminates while they are hardening off. This latter is called 'hot moulding' and Fairey Marine Ltd. of Hamble, Hants, are famous for this form of construction which is extremely tough and impervious to rotting.

You will see that the Wayfarer hull is fairly flat underneath so that she sits on the water with only a small amount of hull immersed—about eight inches would be the greatest depth of the hull skin beneath the surface of the water when she is floating.

The forward area of the boat is called the bow, and the actual sharp junction of the two sides of the hull from deck level to waterline is called the stem. The after area is the stern, and these terms 'bow' and 'stern' apply to the general front and back sections of the boat. At both bow and stern the Wayfarer has a watertight division right across the hull—it is called a bulkhead—which forms the forward and after end of the cockpit space, and these two watertight bulkheads separate off a large airspace at bow and stern which gives the boat a tremendous amount of buoyancy in the event of a capsize.

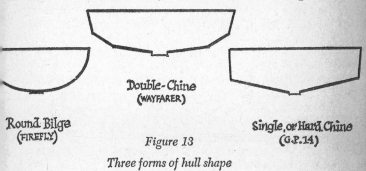

Double-Chine
(WAYFARER)

Round Bilge
(FIREFLY)

Single, or Hard Chine
(G.P.14)

Figure 13

Three forms of hull shape

These watertight tanks are referred to as 'built-in buoyancy' and the Wayfarer does not require any additional buoyancy by way of bags secured in the cockpit: she floats quite adequately in a capsized position on her side with three or four crew sitting up on the side of the boat.

The mast may be of either wood or metal, but in either case the wires which support it will be identical. There are three of these—nearly always of ⅜" circumference stainless steel wire and the one at the bow which braces the mast against a backward thrust is called the forestay. The two (one at either side) which brace the mast against sideways thrust are called shrouds, and you will notice that these shrouds are not attached to the deck of the boat exactly in line with the mast. They are in fact well abaft it, so that they perform the double function of bracing the mast against both sideways and forwards thrust. Some of the larger dinghies, and most yachts, have a fourth wire from the mast to the stern of the boat called a backstay. So you will realise that a stay braces a mast fore-and-aft, whereas a shroud braces it athwartship—across the boat in line with the thwart.

Both shrouds and forestay will have a stainless steel device at their lower ends called a rigging screw (or bottle screw) and this is simply a turnbuckle with opposed screw threads so that by twisting a centre barrel the overall length is either increased or decreased. It follows, since the rigging screw separates the deck from the lower ends of the shrouds and forestay, that if you decrease its length the shrouds etc. will be tightened like a banjo string and vice-versa. This is the means by which a mast is properly 'set up' with exactly the correct amount of slope away from the vertical (this is called the mast rake) and it makes all the difference to the way in which the boat handles.

Collectively the forestay and shrouds form the standing rigging. The running rigging, on the other hand, is the name given to those ropes which hoist the sails and which 'trim' the sails in or out. These are called halyards and sheets respectively.

You will see that a taut wire runs from the boom about a quarter of the way back, down to the foot of the mast. This is the 'kicking strap' and it's there to prevent the boom kicking up into the air when pressure of wind comes on the sail thereby destroying the correct aerofoil shape of the sail. When sailing close hauled with the sail sheeted hard in this kicking strap is largely redundant since the mainsheet is doing most of the work. But as you ease sheets for the boat to 'pay off' across the wind on to the reach or run the kicking strap does its work, for the boom is then no longer being held hard down by the mainsheet.

The centreboard, rather like a knife blade, is housed in a narrow watertight casing called a centreboard case, and the 'plate' pivots on a bolt near its lower forward end. When raised completely the 'plate' does not project at all below the keel of the boat. But as it is lowered—by pulling back on the hand-grips at its upper forward corner—(see Figure 14) the 'plate' arcs down until, when fully lowered, the leading edge is almost vertical.

This centreboard must remain in any position required between fully up and fully down and to effect this there is a

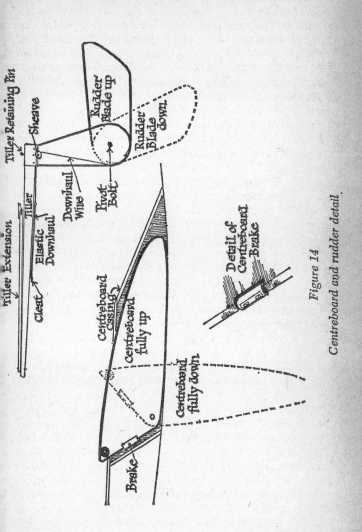

Figure 14

Centreboard and rudder detail.

Labels in figure: Tiller Extension, Tiller Retaining Pin, Sheave, Tiller, Cleat, Elastic Downhaul, Downhaul Wire, Pivot Bolt, Rudder Blade up, Rudder Blade down, Centreboard Casing, Centreboard fully up, Centreboard fully down, Brake, Detail of Centreboard Brake simple brake on the leading edge within the casing. The detail in Figure 14 illustrates this. It consists of a short length of rubber hosepipe screwed through into the end of the centreboard so that when the screws are tightened the hose is squeezed flatter and binds more firmly against the interior faces of the casing. Tension may only be applied by adjusting the screws when the plate is fully lowered. In any other position (other than completely removed from the casing) the screws are inaccessible.

The rudder assembly consists of the rudder blade (pivoted into the rudder stock). This pivoting is necessary in order that the blade may lift up should it hit an obstruction rather than tearing off the rudder hangings. The tiller houses into the rudder hood along the top of the stock, and it is by means of this tiller or helm that one steers the boat. It has an extension arm fixed to its forward end for use when the helmsman is leaning far out. The assembly is completed by an elastic downhaul which simply keeps the pivoted rudder blade from floating up when sailing.

It is very necessary to tension this downhaul immediately one starts sailing, otherwise the rudder blade will rise, and the leverage between the forward end of the tiller and the after end of the rudder blade will soon result in either a rupturing of the rudder stock (see Figure 14) or perhaps a tearing off of the rudder hangings!

It is worth noting this downhaul assembly in detail. A terylene cord runs from the leading edge of the pivoting blade up inside the stock over a sheave and out along the underside of the tiller where it is attached to a stout rubber cord with a metal hook on the end. This hook is stretched forward and engaged with a small cleat attached to the tiller. From Figure 14 you will see that when this tension is applied the pivoting blade is pulled strongly down. On striking the bottom the pivoting blade pushes up and simply stretches the rubber cord. Once in deep water again the tension should snap the blade down, but it is worth checking that this has in fact happened, as there is considerable friction between the blade and the sides of the rudder stock when sailing close hauled. On the run it generally works however. Some dinghies have the reverse arrangement: a rubber cord keeps the blade up, and a second cord has to be tensioned to pull the blade down.

The Wayfarer has a pivoting mast. You can see the pivot bolt between the two uprights either side the mast, but the weight and downward pressure of the mast is not taken on this bolt. The base of the mast seats snugly on a wooden block which takes all the thrust, and the bolt should not take any of the thrust at all. To lower the mast and pivot it backwards one simply detaches the forestay rigging screw, and taking the precaution of having a crew member stand abaft the mast to catch it, gently ease it back keeping a firm hold on the forestay until the crew has the mast well in hand. It may then be lowered gently down to rest on the after deck, taking care to splay out the spreaders (horizontal struts halfway up the mast between shrouds and mast) just before it reaches the deck. Otherwise these will fall down and deflect the mast sideways, thus putting a frightful strain on the pivot bolt.

The distance between the pivot bolt and the forward bulkhead is just great enough for the base of the mast to arc forward as the spar lowers back. It's well worth keeping a wary eye also on the shroud rigging screws as the mast is lowered, because it is possible when the mast falls right back horizontally for these to become bent. The reason for this is that the metal 'chain plates' to which they are attached at deck level (see Figure 12) are orientated athwart the side-decks. In other words they are not angled fore-and-aft so that the rigging screws are only free to arc across the boat (athwartships). But provided a watch is kept on these shroud rigging screws while lowering the spar there is no need to remove them unless the mast is to be taken right out of the boat.

Many dinghies (such as the Enterprise) have the mast base stepped on the deck itself. In this case it is not possible to pivot the spar quickly and raise it again for going under a low bridge. But it is quite easy to unstep the mast and re-step it provided a high wind is not blowing.

In the Wayfarer a stainless steel track called a 'sheet horse' is secured along the top of the transom and in it runs a small 'slide' to which is attached the lower block of the mainsheet assembly. Notice that these pulleys (as a landsman would call them) are referred to as blocks afloat. The upper block is attached to the after end of the boom on a swivel so that the boom may be rotated if necessary—in order to reduce the sail area—without twisting the mainsheet.

The Wayfarer is a very robust boat and has floorboards in the cockpit. These are raised about four inches above the hull skin, and rest on strong bearers so it is permissable to stand inside the boat when she is on a sandy beach, or perhaps a light shingle. In many boats this would be a bad practice as the hull skin is too delicate.

Boats which are used for racing generally have 'toestraps' fitted—strips of terylene webbing secured to the bottom boards or centreboard casing beneath which the crew can tuck their toes in order to facilitate sitting right out over the weather side without falling overboard. For clarity these have not been shown in Figure 12.

Now examine the sails. You will see that the mainsail has a rope sewn into the luff and the foot, and it is this luffrope and footrope which hold the sail into the mast track and boom track respectively. In older types of dinghy there may be a slide sewn into the luff and foot of the sail at about eighteen inch intervals, and these engage with an external track on mast and boom, just like the slide on the sheet horse track, but the newer method is simpler and also more efficient aerodynamically. It causes the absolute minimum disturbance of airflow at the luff.

In the leach of the mainsail are four deep and narrow pockets into which are inserted long thin slivers of wood or plastic called 'sail battens'. These should be removed from the sail after use and stowed carefully otherwise they easily get broken. The batten pockets have a false opening at the leach so that the batten, once fully inserted, may be slid along under a sealed end otherwise they would tend to slip out when sailing. The purpose of these battens is simply to hold the leach rigid and stop it fluttering when sailing. Fluttering causes drag on an airstream and it is conducive to a disturbed airflow. By keeping the leach rigid the used air is allowed to slide cleanly and quickly away. This in turn allows new wind to impinge on the sail, and this means new power.

Before we start to rig the boat, look at the two halyards which are used to hoist the sails (see Figure 4). These emerge from the after side of the mast very near the base, and lead up inside the luff track (not actually inside the hollow of the mast) until the jib halyard emerges from the front side of the mast just below where the shrouds and forestay are attached. The main halyard carries on right up to the top of the mast and emerges very near the 'truck'—the flat top. They both return back down outside the spar and when not in use the lower ends will be secured (probably with a small brass shackle) to some part of the boat within easy reach.

It is important that both halyards have a figure-of-eight knot at their lower end just where they emerge from the base of the mast, otherwise undoubtedly the tail end will get pulled up inside the track and disappear inside the spar. In a metal mast it is fairly easy to re-thread it back out again, but it takes time and is a nuisance. In a wooden spar the halyards often lead up actually inside the hollow spar itself, and it's a frightful business recovering the end of the halyard if once it goes up inside!

As a rule the main halyard is sited to starboard and the jib halyard to port—keep it that way so that you know automatically which halyard hoists which sail.

Now we will rig the boat. You remember this term 'rig' means to set the sails, fit all the equipment required to sail her, and generally get the boat ready in all respects to launch and sail away. Bear in mind that construction and fittings vary slightly in the different classes.

RIGGING THE BOAT

(1) Put in your sail battens, taking care to insert the thin end first and you will find that the top batten is probably shorter than the three lower ones.

(2) Secure the mainsail to the boom. This is done by selecting the clew of the sail, attached to which there will be a length of cord and using this cord to pull with, lead the footrope into the track at the fore end of the boom and pull it back along the track until the brass cringle (eyelet) at the tack coincides with the hole drilled through the boom (or boom fitting) at the fore

end. Insert the tack pin through both boom and tack cringle then slightly tension the foot of the sail by pulling back the clew line and securing it by whatever means is available. On wooden booms this is generally a hole through which the clew line is threaded. It's worth noting that with wooden booms one should take a round turn underneath the boom and back through the clew cringle before knotting the end of the line because you will appreciate that when the sail is sheeted hard in the downward pull on the leach could result in splitting the rather delicate wooden track of the boom. By taking a turn round the boom itself this strain is taken by the spar as a whole and not just on the track.

(3) Select the tack of the jib. On the stemhead fitting you will find shackled a short length of wire called a 'tack strop'. Shackle the tack of the jib to the upper-eye of the tack strop. About every three feet up the luff of the jib you will find jib 'hanks' stoutly secured to the wire which runs up inside the luff of the sail. Secure these to the forestay so that they hold the luff of the jib snug to the forestay. In practice you will soon find that once the jib is hoisted correctly—and that means that the luff is pulled really very tight—the luff wire becomes tauter than the forestay itself. Working your way up the luff from the tack, secure the jib hanks to the forestay ensuring as you do so that you have no twists in the sail. Keep the sail down on deck as you do this. Arriving at the head of the sail, select the jib halyard and be sure it is not twisted round the mast or forestay before shackling it to the head.

(4) Reeve the two jibsheets back through their respective sheetleads. For the jib, these sheets are led inside the shrouds, but if setting the Genoa they go outside the shrouds and back to another separate pair of sheetleads which are positioned more aft on the side decks, to the discomfiture of the crew! Put a figure-of-eight knot in the end of both sheets to prevent accidental unreeving if you let them fly.

(5) Orientate the boat exactly head to wind. This is most important, for if you forget, as soon as you start to hoist sails they will fill and if they do not actually capsize you on the beach, they will foul the shrouds and probably tear as you struggle to get them up.

(6) Both sails are now ready for hoisting, and the first time you rig the boat you will be well advised to do so on a windless day. It will give you time to work it all out without the hazard of a madly flogging sail which can be a little nerve-racking for a complete beginner. I do want to emphasize however that when actually preparing to sail in a brisk wind the sails should NOT be hoisted until you really are completely ready to launch and start sailing. There is more wear and tear suffered by a suit of sails while they flog uselessly on the beach or at a mooring for twenty minutes or so, than months of actual sailing time when the cloth is filled with wind. First get the mainsail up. Ease the wingnut on the gooseneck fitting and slide the gooseneck up to about four inches above the black line painted round the mast at about chest height. Lift the boom and introduce the gooseneck into the square hole at the forward end of the spar. Rest the after end of the boom gently down on the after deck. Gripping the luff near the tack, draw the whole length of the luff through your hands to ensure there are no twists in the sail, and then insert the luff rope at the head into the mast track. Shackle the main halyard to the head of the sail checking that the halyard isn't twisted round the mast, or lying the wrong side of the mast spreaders. Haul on the other end of the halyard while leading the luff into the mast track cleanly. When the sail is nearly hoisted tension will come on to the leach due to the weight of the boom. Get your crew to lift the after end of the spar as you hoist the last three feet or so—it will make it a lot easier. When the sail is snug up to the top of the mast as high as it will go, belay the halyard on to the adjacent starboard cleat.

(7) Don't mess about now. If there is any wind at all that main will be flogging, and every flip of those battens is a penny out of your pocket for sail repairs and eventual replacement! Ease off the wing nut on the gooseneck and 'swig' the tack down until the foot of the sail (and that does not mean the underside of the boom) is not lower than the black line round the mast. This stretches the luff. Lock the wing nut again to keep it under tension. Coil the loose halyard up neatly and stow it where it will not get in the way when sailing.

(8) Set up the kicking strap. Insert the key into the slot at the

lower edge of the boom and pull the assembly tight. This keeps the boom from lifting.

(9) Hoist the jib by hauling on the jib halyard and belay this on the adjacent cleat to Port. It's very important that the luff of the jib is as tight as you can get it, otherwise the performance of the boat (particularly when beating) will suffer. Make sure that both jibsheets and the mainsheet are completely free to run once the sails are hoisted. If they become foul and 'snarl' up a sharp change of wind can easily result in chaos or capsize.

(10) Assuming the above to have been completed at the water's edge, now haul the boat into the water until she is floating. The crew must hold on to the bow in order to keep her roughly head to wind once she is afloat.

(11) Ship the rudder, i.e. fix it in its position for use. The Wayfarer, as you will have seen, has a folding rudder blade which enables it to be shipped while in shallow water or when actually on the beach. Lift the blade up and engage the two hangings—pintle and gudgeon—with the corresponding hangings on the boat's transom. You will find that the lower hangings will engage about a quarter of an inch before the upper ones which makes it very much easier to ship. See that the rudder stock is housed snug down on the transom hangings before attempting to insert the tiller beneath the sheethorse and into the rudder hood. Make sure that the rudder blade downhaul (often called the 'shock cord') is lying in the groove provided at the rudder head before inserting the tiller, otherwise the latter will not slide home properly. Don't attempt to attach the 'shock cord' elastic to the cleat on the tiller until you are in deep enough water, otherwise you will simply be forcing the blade down into the sand or shingle.

(12) Check that your mainsheet is not twisted and that there is a figure-of-eight knot in the end in such a position that it jams the lower block just before the boom can rub against either shroud when eased fully out for the running position. Ensure that the watertight hatches at fore and after buoyancy tanks are properly secured, that all the bungs are in bulkheads and transom, and that the centreboard retaining pin is removed so that the 'plate' may be lowered. Provided you are wearing a lifejacket—and your crew—away you go!

SAILING FROM A LEE SHORE

A lee shore is where the wind is blowing on to the shore, and if the water is shallow near the beach it's the most difficult shore to sail away from. Let's think why.

It is evident that in order to leave a lee shore one will have to sail as close to the wind as possible—in fact one will have to sail close hauled in order to leave the shore at all should the wind be blowing on to the beach at right-angles to the water-line. This point of sailing demands that the centreboard is lowered fully in order to prevent leeway, but this is impossible on a shallow beach! One has to compromise.

Watch any experienced dinghy sailor leaving a beach under these conditions and you will probably see him do the following:

(a) Direct his crew to wade into the water and hold the boat's bow into the eye of the wind.

(b) Position himself at the stern of the dinghy which will now be completely afloat; he will probably place both hands on the transom—his feet in the water of course, not in the boat—and momentarily holding the boat head-to-wind he will order his crew to jump aboard and stand by to ease the centreboard gently down, taking care NOT to stab it right into the sea-bed otherwise the whole operation will come to a grinding halt and the boat will almost certainly end up on the shoreline!

(c) The helmsman will now give the boat a mighty shove, angling her bow slightly to one side the wind line. At the last moment he will jump aboard, grab the helm and harden in the mainsheet at the same time steering the boat to about 45 degrees from the eye of the wind. The crew will now be lowering the plate as far as possible so that the boat will quickly get a grip on the water and enable her to be worked to windward clear of the beach.

The boat will now be sailing close hauled with jib flogging; since the crew is concentrating totally on intelligently lowering the centreboard, and it is this latter, coupled with competent sailing on the helmsman's part, that makes the difference between getting off that lee shore or ending up back on it again.

What happens is this: the boat, forging ahead almost into the eye of the wind under the impetus of the push given by the helmsman, is getting into water which though not yet deep, is just deep enough for the centreboard to drop to a point where it will grip the water sufficiently to enable the dinghy to start sailing.

At first of course she will make leeway quite a lot but with competent helming she will nevertheless make some way up to windward—enough to get into deeper water. With the gradual lowering of the 'plate' the boat sails more and more efficiently. Finally, with the 'plate' right down the crew can harden the jibsheet and you're away close hauled.

That is what should happen. Often it doesn't and it's not only the inexperienced chap who ends up back ashore again: it's not quite as easy as it sounds.

The choice of tack is important. If the wind is blowing slightly more along the shore than dead on to it, always choose

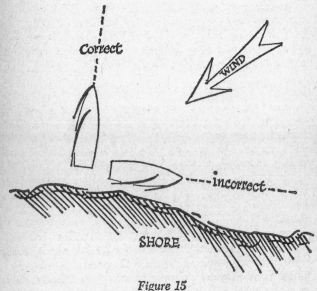

Figure 15

Choosing the correct tack from a lee shore

the tack (port or starboard) which results in your leaving shore at the greatest angle. This is common sense: in Figure 15 you would certainly not try to sail off the lee shore on port tack otherwise you would simply sail slap along the beach, hitting any other craft which might be there!

So much for the experienced sailor. There are other ways of doing it. For instance if you have a paddle or pair of oars you can row or paddle off into deep water with sails already set but sheets free until you are in deep enough water for the plate to be lowered. Then it's just a case of the helmsman sailing the boat gently until the crew has stowed the paddle or oars and can attend to the jib.

Alternatively you may choose to 'kedge' yourself out into deep water by throwing out the anchor to windward and rapidly pulling the dinghy up to it, then repeating the process. This is quite quick and efficient but it does take a bit of practice to throw that anchor well to windward without hooking the blessed thing either in the shrouds, forestay, or yourself. I've seen great fun ensue when the helmsman started sailing the boat before the anchor was brought back aboard! It can then get wrapped round the centreboard so that the latter can neither be raised nor the anchor recovered.

SAILING FROM A WEATHER SHORE

In this case the wind is blowing you off the shore and it's very easy. Quite the reverse conditions now apply to when sailing off a lee shore, for there is no hurry to lower the plate since you need to run before the wind in order to leave the shore at all and the plate is not therefore required.

Simply 'back' the jib by pulling it out to one side—it matters not which side if the wind is dead offshore. Immediately the bow will swing away from the eye of the wind, and away from the shore.

Provided the mainsheet is eased completely the boat will proceed to run down wind goosewinged if required until she is in deep enough water to lower the plate and slice away on a reach or any other point of sailing you wish. A difficulty which may arise when sailing off a weather shore is in the case of the crew lowering the plate too soon. This can result in the boat 'rounding up' (swinging round into the wind) and nosing back on shore again with the plate being pushed up by the beach. This is only likely to happen if the helmsman has not eased the mainsheet enough and is not paying attention to his steering, but you will appreciate that the boat tends to pivot round the centreboard and swing up head to wind if she is not prevented.

Once offshore and catching the full force of the wind you must be on your guard against an accidental gybe. Remember that you will be running fairly well down wind so it's necessary to watch your course carefully and not become disorientated— a disorientated helmsman is a menace to himself and everybody else in the vicinity!

GETTING THE FEEL OF THE BOAT

This matter of orientation relative to the wind is, frankly, the most difficult thing to master for the complete beginner. At risk of repeating myself I'll again emphasize that EVERYTHING you do in a boat once afloat is related to the invisible wind line, and the angle your sails are making to the wind means the difference between being in control of the boat or being thrown completely off balance and probably into the water.

The difficulty is one cannot see the wind so it's all done by feel. To give you an idea of what I mean by this, imagine you're in a Wayfarer with me. The wind is brisk—not too strong but brisk enough to make her speed and capsize her too, if mishandled.

Assume we are sailing on the port tack, at about 55 degrees off the wind which is not close hauled but would be referred to as a close or fine reach. The plate will be right down on this point of sailing and we will both be sitting on the weather side with our feet tucked beneath the toestraps—leaning out just as much as is necessary to keep her nearly vertical but not quite. She should be heeling about five to ten degrees away from the wind. I have the tiller (or tiller extension if more convenient) in my right hand because that is the hand nearest to the tiller. The mainsheet is in my left hand and I'm taking good care to see that the loose end of the mainsheet is free to run and not fouled on anything such as my feet or the tiller itself. You will be sitting fairly well forward toward the bow with the lee jib-sheet in hand and the weather sheet (this will be the port sheet) left completely loose.

For a moment bring your body in towards the centre line of the boat and I will do the same, because I'm going to gently ease the mainsheet and want you to do the same with the jib-sheet until both sails are flogging uselessly. It was necessary for us both to move towards the centre line of the boat because, had we not done so as we eased the sheets, due to our weight on the weather side she would have heeled to windward. We have deliberately 'spilled wind' from both our sails and the pressure in them has gone. The boat will hardly move forward at all. In effect we've taken the foot off the accelerator and thrown her out of gear.

Now watch what happens as I begin to sheet in the main. First notice that while I'm sheeting the sail in, I carefully steer the boat on her selected course, in this case a close reach. I do this by drawing the sheet in with my left hand and then locking it beneath my thumb against the tiller extension which I'm holding in my right hand. But I do not waggle the tiller. It takes practice, but after a bit both your hands act quite independently, one to haul in the sheet and one to momentarily lock it while carefully steering the boat. As the sail is sheeted more towards the fore-and-aft line of the boat, so the leach fills with wind first, then progressively fills more and more towards the luff until finally the luff itself ceases to flog and AT THIS EXACT POINT I cease to harden the sheet any more because now, and only now, the sail is giving the maximum possible thrust forward provided the wind direction remains constant. If it doesn't, then of course I shall have to re-trim the mainsail until this exact point where the luff is not quite 'lifting' as they say.

The same applies to the jib. You gently sheet it in until the luff has just stopped 'lifting'. As we sheeted in both sails, so the boat started moving forward and our combined weights had to move farther and farther out over the weather side of the boat to offset the increasing pressure in the sails. Otherwise she would heel too far to leeward and probably dip the lee side-deck beneath the water: the last stage before a capsize! Your body and mine are movable weights which must be kept in just the correct position to ensure that the boat remains nearly vertical.

This angle of heel, slightly to leeward, is important because then the full height of the sails are presented to the wind and after striking the sail and being deflected the used wind can

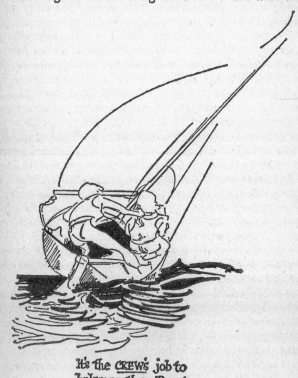

It's the CREW's job to balance the Boat.

escape cleanly off the leach. One thing we must try to avoid is heeling the boat to windward. If this occurs the wind is deflected down instead of more or less horizontally away, and results in a bag of dead air just to windward of the boat which is useless. But conversely she must not be allowed to heel too far to leeward otherwise the sails will begin to spill the wind by presenting too slanting an angle in the vertical plane. It may look and feel dramatic but the boat will not go so fast for half the power of the wind is being thrown away, quite apart from the hull form of the boat presenting the wrong shape to the water, and the centreboard skidding like mad due to its wrong angle of presentation. The designer intended her to be sailed more or less upright so try to keep her that way.

I'm going to angle the boat more across the wind until it is blowing exactly at right angles to her fore-and-aft line. This is often referred to as a 'beam reach' because the wind is now said to be blowing on to the 'beam' of the boat. I trim my mainsail accordingly, and you trim your jib. A beam reach is one of the fastest points of sailing with any given wind force, because the thrust from the sails is now almost exactly in line with the direction in which the boat is heading. Because she travels fast in a brisk wind on a beam reach the plate can be brought about half up. You see, water is a very dense medium. The faster an object travels through it, the greater will it's resistance become—if you think of a water skier actually standing on the water you will understand this. It is only possible because he is travelling at some twenty to thirty knots that he stays on the surface. Slow down and he begins to sink.

So it is with the centreboard of a boat. The faster the plate moves through the water, the more resistant to leeway does the water become, and if a smaller area of plate will do the job adequately there is a disadvantage in keeping it down any more than required, for it merely forms more drag in the water. The less drag the better so bring it half up in brisk winds, but in light airs keep it right down otherwise you'll make a lot of leeway even on a beam reach.

Provided I keep the boat exactly on course and the wind remains constant we will now get the maximum possible drive from both sails since they're trimmed correctly. But if, due to lack of attention, you sheet your jib in more than is necessary, you will cause the airstream off the weather side of your sail to be deflected too sharply which will bring it on to the lee side of my mainsail luff. This is fatal: it completely destroys the speed-up of the airstream to leeward of my main thus destroying a large part of the drive of my sail. Watch the luff of your jib like a hawk: keep that sail trimmed at all times (except when running) so that the luff is not QUITE lifting—and the most important word there is 'QUITE'. The same applies to my mainsail. It's very true to say that a boat when close hauled or on a reach is literally sailed by the luff of her sails.

So much for the reach: now I'm going to direct the boat more toward the wind so that we shall be sailing close hauled. I gently ease the helm 'down'. That means down wind—away from me toward the lee side of the boat. As the helm goes down the rudder pivots the opposite way and the boat therefore commences to turn up wind (to port). The plate must now be fully lowered. I emphasize here that the helm movements must be carried out smoothly with no jerking. Every time the helm is jerked the boat slows a little and the rudder hangings throw away another hour or so of life!

The boat now turns up wind and instantly the luff of both main and jib start lifting. Power is now being lost, so simultaneously with the turning of the boat we both harden our sheets until the luff again is not quite lifting. I continue to turn the boat until both main and jibsheets are hardened right in. From now on, if I continue to turn the boat towards the eye of the wind there will be nothing more I can do about it with regard to the sheets: the luff of the sails will lift away because the sheets are as hard in as possible.

This is sailing close hauled, and any further adjustment of the sail angle to the wind line has to be done with the helm by turning the boat just so as to keep the luffs not quite lifting. It may not look anything like 45 degrees to the wind line from the burgee at the top of the mast, but remember this burgee shows the apparent wind, which is different from the true wind. The boat is moving forward so the wind appears to draw ahead the faster she moves. Nothing is quite as it appears to be! It's all relative.

SPILLING WIND AND LUFFING UP

Here I wish to underline the difference between spilling wind and luffing up. When sailing on a reach any sudden strengthening of the wind force may heel the boat to leeward so that it is necessary to reduce pressure in the sails by easing sheets. This is called spilling wind because the sails do just that—wind is deliberately spilled, particularly from the upper areas of the sails. The course of the boat however has remained unaltered.

Exactly the same effect may be obtained by altering the course of the boat more towards the wind without easing sheets. This latter manoeuvre is called luffing up. You may wonder whether one tactic is to be preferred to the other, and the answer depends on the situation at the time. If your course is taking you directly to your destination and you are not having to beat to windward to get there, it will be advantageous to spill wind in the gusts in order to keep her upright.

If however your destination is to windward of your course when sailing close hauled, then there is an obvious advantage in luffing up since by so doing you are both easing the wind pressure in the sails and also gaining ground to windward—towards your destination. You will soon find however that as a means of easing pressure in your sails, luffing up is a slower manoeuvre. What is more, as the boat turns she tends to heel a little more to leeward in the first stage of the turn, so frequently a helmsman will combine a little of both tactics: luffing up and spilling wind at the same time.

The great thing is not to overdo either manoeuvre or the result will be disconcerting to the crew, for in both cases the boat will tend to heel violently to windward. Unless helmsman and crew are very quick to respond by shifting their weights inboard towards the centreline of the boat they may be pitched into the water backwards.

HOW TO TACK

Now let us tack, or 'go about', both of which terms mean the same thing. We are sailing close hauled on the port tack and wish to bring her round head to wind and beyond until we are sailing close hauled on starboard tack. My preparatory warning to you, my crew, is 'Ready about!' This simply warns you that very shortly I intend to tack. The only action required by you is to ensure that your jibsheet is not jammed in the cleat which may be positioned just inboard of the sheetlead. To effect this unjamming you smartly jerk your sheet in and upwards which snaps it out of the jam cleat's jaw.

When I see you have unjammed your sheet I give the order 'Lee-ho!' which is an abbreviation for the words, 'I am now putting my helm to leeward'. I ease the helm gently down at the same time folding the tiller extension aft along the arm of the tiller. As the boat comes upright and the boom commences to swing across we both move gently across the boat—you facing forward as you do so, myself facing aft. We take care to balance the boat perfectly as she luffs up head to wind and then tacks beyond the eye of the wind until she fills on the starboard tack. By now we should be sitting out over the weather side again and we have turned through roughly 90 degrees.

As we passed across the boat it was necessary to duck beneath the boom, and in addition you probably found that the kicking strap tried to chop off your head. You'll soon get used to coping with these hazards. Just as the boat's head was in the eye of the wind (but not before) you 'let fly' your starboard jibsheet and gently hardened in the port jibsheet so that by the time I had settled on the new tack your jib was correctly sheeted in. If you timed this right the jib would hardly have flogged for more than one instant during the tack, and will have been working all the time. For myself, as I put the helm down at the start of the tack I momentarily let it go and took the sheet in my right hand (which previously had been holding the tiller), switching my left hand on to the tiller or its extension depending on the strength of the wind. This change-over of hands on sheet and tiller was affected as I moved across the boat, facing aft. At no time did I bring the tiller extension forward. It simply folded back toward the stern and out over the opposite side as she filled on Starboard tack.

Come aft now, and take the helm from me. I'll spill wind a little in order to allow the boat to remain upright as we change positions, it makes it a lot easier for us.

We are on starboard tack. Take the tiller in your left hand and hold the mainsheet in your right hand. Disregard the jib: I'll look after that. Keeping the boat steady on course sheet the mainsail gently in until the luff is no longer 'lifting'. As you do this do you feel the tiller trying to pull away from you—down to leeward? In order to prevent this you have to put tension on it towards you—to weather—otherwise the boat will swing head-to-wind. This need to pull the helm constantly toward you when sailing is called 'carrying weather helm' and the boat is deliberately designed so that she does carry a slight amount of weather helm because, if left to her own devices she will then automatically 'luff up' and stop sailing.

Experiment with the tiller. Pull it gently towards you and watch the bow swing to port, away from the eye of the wind as you do so. Notice how she immediately heels more to leeward due to the greater angle of incidence of wind on your sails. Now swing the bow back toward the wind by easing the helm down (away from you) just until the luff of the sail shows signs of lifting. Keep her steady on that course.

Look up to weather—on your starboard bow. Do you see that darker ruffling of the water surface up there? That means you can expect a stronger gust of wind, and since that's the direction from which the wind is coming we may expect it to hit us at any moment. Be ready to spill wind if necessary should the boat heel too violently, but at the same time be careful to keep the boat steady on course. This isn't as easy as it sounds, for just as the wind hits the sails and you're concentrating on easing your sheet, so the boat tries to swing up toward the eye of the wind and you must simultaneously correct this tendency by applying more weather helm. It results in a sort of scissor movement between sheet and tiller. One hand eases the sheet out while the other pulls the tiller up. Meanwhile of course we are both adjusting our weights to effect a constant angle of heel. You'll wish you had two heads!

Now pay off the wind on to a reach: pull the helm up towards you and as the bow swings off the wind we both ease sheets so that the luffs of our sails are maintaining exactly the same angle with the wind as before. As the boat continues swinging gently round to the beam reach position she will accelerate, and as we swing yet further so that we commence running on a broad reach our weights will need to be brought more into the cockpit of the boat because the wind pressure is now more toward the bow of the boat.

RUNNING

Take care here. Turn the boat very gently down wind and I

will raise the plate until it is nearly fully up. Watch the burgee at the masthead and when it is streaming out over the bow keep the boat steady on that course and do not allow her to swing round any more. My jib has now collapsed because it is now sheltered from the wind by the mainsail, so I let fly my port jibsheet and sheet in on starboard to set the sails goose-winged. Often a short pole called a 'jib stick' or 'whisker pole' is set between the clew of the jib and the mast to stretch this sail out when running goosewinged. It keeps the jib using every available bit of wind it can.

We are now travelling comparatively slowly though this can be misleading: it's never quite as slowly as it looks—the wake astern will confirm this. Remember that we are running with the wind and therefore our relative windspeed is reduced by our own speed over the bottom, and in addition both sails are completely stalled. It's worth noting too that the ripples on the surface of the water are moving in the same direction as our-selves, and this can give a misleading impression of being almost stopped.

You will have noticed that as we began to run before the wind I moved my weight to the opposite side to which you are sitting, and it will be better if we both move aft a little in order to counteract the downward thrust on the bow of the boat caused by the pressure of wind from right aft. If the bow is allowed to 'plough' (dig in deep) due to too much weight being forward, it will slow the boat a lot. Avoid over correcting how-ever, for if our weights are brought too far aft the transom will dig causing suction which similarly tends to slow the boat.

DISTRIBUTION OF WEIGHT

Weight distribution in a dinghy is of vital importance and can make just that difference between winning and coming in second! In general, when sailing close hauled the crew and helmsman should ease well forward. The more one comes off the wind toward the run, the more one's weight must come aft. It's a matter of feeling the boat, and varies with different classes. Every moment that you are on that helm you are feeding in information through your sense of touch and balance and it won't be long before you automatically respond to the needs of the boat. You will develop a really fast co-ordination of mind and muscle.

We are now running goosewinged on starboard tack, for although the wind is not blowing on either port or starboard side, nevertheless the mainsail is out to port, so technically we are still on starboard tack.

You will understand why this definition is important when we come to consider the Regulations for Preventing Collision at Sea—the 'Rules of the Road' for sailing boats.

HOW TO GYBE

The wind is fairly light so let's practice a gybe. To do this you have only to swing the bow to port so as to bring the wind on to the other side of your mainsail and both sail and boom will blow across with gusto. Unless you can tell exactly when this is about to happen you will probably receive a blow on the head—not to mention a possible capsize in strong winds. The sudden shift of pressure from out over the port side where the mainsail was, to out over the starboard side where the sail will be after the gybe, can result in a violent lurch. Unless we are quick to respond by counterbalancing her with our weights, we may easily capsize. In fact I think more capsizes are caused through inadvertent gybing than any other factor in sailing. Weight is useful in a boat provided it's in the right place, and to be in the right place needs quick response and accuracy. Let's gybe carefully and under control!

The tiller movement is exactly the opposite to that of tacking. First ensuring that you are in fact pointing the boat straight down wind, pull the helm gently toward you. At the same time I will 'hand the boom across'. By this I mean that I will start the boom on its way across the boat before it is really ready to go. Once the wind gets the other side of the leach of course it will carry on of its own accord—and it is at this moment, just as the sail slams across and fills with wind on the starboard side of the boat that two instantaneous reactions must take place. (1) You must apply just enough weather helm to prevent the boat from 'rounding up' head to wind, and (2) both our weights must counterbalance the new pressure point on the starboard side of the boat caused by the new position of the mainsail.

This is something that will only come with practice and my bet is that your first few gybes in any wind worth mentioning will be exciting affairs.

BROACHING

One point there I would like to explain more fully. Immediately after the gybe has taken place, your reaction on the helm must be to counteract the tendency of the boat to turn up into the wind. Should you have forgotten to raise your plate when running, this tendency will be much more marked—indeed in strong winds it can become quite uncontrollable. The boat will swing away from the mainsail (in the opposite direction to which the mainsail is set) thus presenting her beam to the wind. It results in a violent lurch to leeward and this is called 'broaching'. It's caused by the sudden shift in pressure from the changed sail position which makes the boat pivot round her plate, and must be anticipated and avoided by applying the necessary amount of weather helm before it actually happens. By so doing you can keep the boat's bow pointing down wind after the gybe has taken place.

We have now sailed on all points of sailing and carried out a tack and a gybe, but there are two more manoeuvres I would like to perform with you before we beach the dinghy again. Firstly, I want you to take 'way off' the boat. In other words stop her moving through the water—but we have no brakes!

GETTING IN IRONS

The best means of achieving this is to luff up head to wind and hold the boat there with the helm so that the sails are flogging. For a while the momentum of boat and crew will keep her ranging up into the eye of the wind, but she will soon come to a halt. Once you have stopped moving through the water your rudder becomes useless and you are said to be 'in irons'. You won't remain in irons long however hard you try, for as soon as the boat starts moving backwards through the water she will swing across the wind one way or the other and you will have to be alert to avoid capsizing before she starts sailing again.

Secondly, I want to actually capsize with you, doing the thing in slow motion as it were.

WHEN IT REALLY HAPPENS: CAPSIZE AND RECOVERY

I've explained in Chapter 1 that the capsize is more often than not a comparatively gentle affair, and remarked that whether you remained dry on top of the boat or immersed alongside it in the water is largely a question of how agile and fit you are, and how quick your responses have become to the movements of the boat.

Let me take the helm again and I'll deliberately capsize her to leeward. To do this I'm going to ask you to cleat your jib-sheet. We are sailing close hauled and I am going to tack, but I want you to ignore my preparatory order 'ready about' and leave your jibsheet cleated. When I tack I am going to do deliberately what a beginner often does quite by accident: I'm going to make the boat swing through the eye of the wind and then let her continue swinging much too far right across the wind and keep my mainsheet hard in. The combined effect of your jib being back-winded (sheeted in to weather) and my mainsail remaining sheeted far too hard is quite enough to put her over. So here we go:

'Ready about?'

'Lee-Ho!'

She swings head to wind, passes through the eye of the wind, sped on her way across by your back-winded jib and turns slam across the wind. This is it! The boat digs her lee side-deck under the water, and gently sags down until mast and sails slap on to the surface. The centreboard is now sticking out horizontally just above the surface, and let's imagine you have fallen into the water and are holding on to the mast just below the boom. I've managed to scramble up on top of the hull and am sitting astride it with one leg down either side. Your instinctive reaction will be to join me up here and get clear of the water again, and to do this you will almost certainly put one foot on the centreboard case which forms a handy step, place the other on the mast, and grab the rubbing strake above to start levering yourself up. Unless you are very quick in doing this you'll only succeed in levering the mast and sails down into the water so that they begin to plumb the depths, which makes it progressively more difficult for you to get up on top, and results in an ever increasing tendency for the boat to turn turtle with mast vertically down.

Unless the water is deeper than the inverted mast you stand a good chance of breaking the latter on the bottom, and even if the water is deep enough it's quite a bit more difficult to get the boat righted again from this turn turtle position than if we had tackled the job when the boat was merely on her side!

WATCH THE MAST AND PRESS
GENTLY DOWN ON THE CENTREPLATE

So frankly, if you haven't moved quickly enough to get on top of the hull as she capsized you might just as well remain in the water, taking care not to get separated from the boat, while I get on with the business of righting her.

I find it easiest to effect this by placing one foot only down on the centreboard, keeping the other foot up on the rubbing strake, and gripping the rubbing strake with both hands. I then lean gently backwards so as to lever the boat upwards. You will appreciate that this is fruitless if you (in the water) are holding on to the mast. My weight pressing gently on the plate has got to lift the mast and drag both sails out of the water, and I always watch the mast carefully while doing this because while in the early stages of righting the boat there is a great deal of suction from the water acting on the sail as it begins to drag free of the surface, once this adhesion is broken the righting process accelerates rapidly, and a critical point is soon reached where, unless I'm very quick to spring up and into the cockpit, the whole blessed boat will arc up and over and capsize toward me again. In which case we're both in the water!

So, as the boat comes upright, I leap back into the cockpit, let fly the jibsheet which was jammed prior to the capsize, and commence to bail with the large plastic bucket kept aboard for the purpose. In the meantime you hold on to the stem of the boat by the forestay so that she remains headed into the wind as I bail her dry. When she is sufficiently emptied to commence sailing again I will give you a hand to come back to the transom of the boat and help you inboard over the stern. This getting inboard has to be done as quickly as possible because as soon as your body in the water moves to the stern of the boat, she will tend to swing off the wind—and if you remain there she will commence running down wind dragging you astern, and there won't be much I can do about it either until you are inboard! So get in quickly if you can.

If you can't, I shall put you back at the bow again so that the boat swings once more head to wind. Then I shall lower the sails and after that we can take our time in getting you aboard over the stern.

GETTING BACK ABOARD FROM THE WATER

You may think I'm putting too much emphasis on this getting aboard after a capsize, but it is not too easy, and from experience I have found it is only a fit person who can lift himself by his arms alone up on to the after deck of the boat—or into the cockpit if there is no after deck. You appreciate that there is nothing against which you can press your feet and it all has to be done by the arms. But there is a knack in it. Your lifejacket can help enormously. Take a firm grip of the transom with both hands, inhale deeply, and shove yourself vertically down in the water still gripping the transom. Now pull yourself up as hard as you possibly can, and you'll find that the combined buoyancy of your jacket plus your inflated lungs will give just that extra impetus to your lift which enables you to fall forward over the transom into the boat.

If between us we find it quite impossible to get you back aboard I shall ask you to turn with your back to the transom and pass the end of my mainsheet (which is no longer in use) beneath your armpits to hold you snugly there. If the shore to leeward is safe to land on I'll then run quietly down under jib alone until you can start walking again and get the whole thing sorted out.

Proportional to the physical fitness.

But if the wind is blowing us offshore I shall anchor the boat provided the water is shallow enough. If it's too deep then we both have to do everything we can to retard our rate of drift offshore, and this can best be done by shoving the mainsail and boom over the side into the water and trailing it—plus you— from the bow so that the boat can remain head to wind thus offering the minimum resistance. In the Wayfarer I would also lower the mast thereby further reducing the wind resistance. After that, it's a question of waiting for the rescue launch. But I do emphasize that to have been sailing off a weather shore at sea would have been very foolish and unseamanlike in the first place unless a suitable power boat was in attendance. One just does not get oneself into such a situation if one approaches this sailing game in a responsible fashion.

Before leaving this capsize I had better mention one rather obvious aid when righting the boat. It is, of course, very much easier to get her upright again if the sails are first lowered while she is still capsized. In addition, when she has been righted there's not so much chance of capsizing immediately again due to wind in the sails. But frankly, most modern dinghies have so much built-in buoyancy that you can virtually carry on sailing the moment she is righted while the crew get on with bailing out the water.

I don't want to get morbid about this, but we have now dealt with the most likely event in sailing a dinghy that could lead to a tragedy. Before leaving the subject I'll again express my opinion that the risk of serious mishap is almost inversely proportional to the physical fitness of the person involved. The ability to move quickly and with agility, to have good co-ordination of mind and muscle, and to keep one's head when the unexpected happens, can make the difference between an exciting and laughable adventure, or tragedy.

RETURNING TO LEE AND WEATHER SHORES

Before actually beaching the boat, no matter if this be on a weather or lee shore, we will obviously wish to take way off the dinghy—to stop, that is. Not to do so is rather like driving a car into the garage with one's foot on the accelerator: one stops alright, but it could be disastrous!

Think first of returning to a weather shore. The wind is blowing from the shoreline to you so it's a very simple manoeuvre. You sail close hauled until near the beach—perhaps thirty feet or so away—and then (making sure one has sufficient momentum to carry the boat up into the eye of the wind) luff up and bring the plate right up. The boat, with both sails spilling wind, ranges slowly up on to the beach and the crew jumps ashore to hold her head to wind while you lower sails and unship the rudder.

Approaching a lee shore on the other hand is more difficult. Obviously one cannot simply run down on to the beach or you'll hit it with full power on. But of course to luff-up in order to spill wind will be to head the boat away from the beach and you certainly will not beach her satisfactorily stern-first! So if the wind is blowing directly on to shore the best method is to luff-up about twenty yards offshore and drop the mainsail, then run slowly in under jib alone.

If however the wind is at an angle to the lee shore one may

choose to beach by selecting the tack which brings the boat closest to the wind—the tack which is nearest to being close-hauled—and on nearing the beach let fly both main and jib to switch off all power. Bring the centreboard right up and steer the boat parallel to the shoreline. Without the lateral resistance of the plate the boat will drift sideways until she touches the beach, and the crew should immediately back-wind the jib and cleat it there before jumping out. By so doing it is ensured that the bow of the boat is pinned on to the beach, otherwise she might well continue to range along the shoreline and hit the next boat there, if there is one! Remember that a dinghy left without the jib back-winded in such circumstances will be tending to swing her bow up into the eye of the wind because of the slight thrust of the mainsail. She can easily sail offshore on her own, or at least range along the shoreline doing damage to herself and anything else in the way. Get the sails down as quickly as possible.

Remember too, that it's advisable on reaching the beach to take tension off the rudder downhaul otherwise the blade will be digging hard down into the sand, and if a well meaning volunteer shoves you stern-first off the beach again those rudder hangings will be badly strained, if not broken off completely. If you intend leaving the boat for more than a few minutes you should lower the sails, unship the rudder, and put an anchor ashore or leave someone in charge to see that the boat does not drift away. Actually this is unlikely unless the wind shifts, after all it's a lee shore we're beached on, but it's better to be wise than sorry!

SAILING FROM A NON-TIDAL MOORING

If a dinghy is secured to a mooring by the bow in non-tidal water, she will always lie head-to-wind which makes it possible to get on with rigging the sails. On stepping from the tender or launch which has taken you from shore to the dinghy take great care to step into the dinghy as near to her centreline as possible, and never on to the side-deck otherwise she'll heel alarmingly. Keep the boat stable by remaining amidships as you 'bend on' the sails. This term 'bend on' by the way comes from the days when sails were actually lashed to spars on square riggers, and it covers the whole operation of actually hoisting the sails and seeing that they are properly set. The boat will lie quietly head to wind while you are doing this, being tethered, as it were, by the nose.

When all is ready to cast off the mooring lower the centre-board and instruct your crew to cast off the buoy, avoiding if possible standing on the foredeck as he does so. In fact once the sails are hoisted it's not advisable to stand in a dinghy at any time since by so doing the centre of gravity of the whole unit —man and boat—is raised greatly and makes it more unstable.

If you have a choice of tacks on which to leave the mooring, decide which you intend using and get the crew to back-wind the jib accordingly. For example, if you propose leaving on starboard tack you will tell your crew immediately on casting off to back-wind the jib to starboard. This pushes the bow to port, and when the boat is sufficiently angled across the wind for the mainsail to draw, harden both sheets on the lee side, and away you go.

To pick up the mooring again you have simply to bear in mind that you will need to be nearly stopped when you reach the buoy otherwise you will overshoot it, and if your crew is manfully holding on to the buoy you will probably overshoot him as well!

View your mooring from well away and decide on your best angle of approach relative to the wind and any obstructions which may present themselves. The ideal approach to a non-tidal mooring is to sail on a reach from a position down-wind, and when about three boats' lengths directly to leeward of the buoy luff up head to wind at the same time giving the order 'let fly sheets'. The sails, being slack, will then cease to influence the boat and you simply steer her so as to bring the buoy up neatly to the bow, informing your crew which bow you propose to use. The position of your fairlead at the stem will influence this. Your crew should be leaning forward to grasp the buoy as soon as possible and immediately he does so he should bring the buoyrope in through the fairlead at the bow, securing the buoy inboard, or alternatively take the boat's painter (rope lanyard) through the fairlead and reeve it through the eye on top of the buoy. This all depends on the type of mooring. Some buoys are intended to be made fast inboard, others are intended to be left in the water and have a line from the boat secured to them.

The essential thing is that the boat is secured from her stem, and from no other point. She will then lie head to wind and you can get on with dropping your sails in safety. Once secured

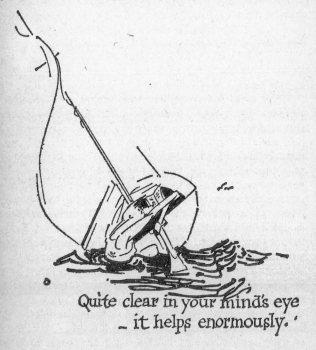

Quite clear in your mind's eye
_ it helps enormously. '

to the mooring get both main and jib down as quickly as possible and don't forget to raise the centreboard and lock it in the up position with the retaining pin!

Before you carry on reading I would like you to re-read these practical examples, linking them with the theory in Chapter One and making certain that it's quite clear in your mind's eye what is happening and why it is happening. It will help enormously when you eventually get out there in the boat.

3

Seamanship

EVOLUTION OF SAIL SHAPES AND TYPES OF RIG

This is an interesting study in itself. To start it all, I suppose there was a hairy caveman sitting on a log. It's a pretty ghastly supposition, but I'll bet it's accurate, and it would not be long before our hirsute hero augments his natural air resistant shagginess by grabbing a handy bush and holding it aloft. He would soon tumble to the fact that this speeded up his progress by merely offering more resistance to the wind. For ages, in certain areas of the world, the concept of a sail relied upon the same basic assumption: namely that a sail caught the wind and more or less blew the boat in the same direction as the wind. So we have the development of the squaresail which was bent on to a spar called a yard slung at right angles to the mast, and it's a fair guess that our modern word 'halyard' originated from 'haul yard' since the first squaresails were hoisted by means of hauling up the yard to which they were bent.

After a while sailors realised that they could sail not only dead before the wind, but by bracing the yard—that means swinging the yard one way or the other—they could continue to sail almost across the wind. If they were on starboard tack then the port end of the yard would be swung aft. The starboard (i.e. weather end) would therefore swing forward and the sail would remain almost at right angles to the wind direction even though the boat herself was angled across the wind. One can trace the process of sail development beginning from this first simple action.

Trying frequently to sail nearer to the wind—that means at

less of an angle to the wind line—the skipper of a square rigger would find constantly that the weather edge of his squaresail was the one part of the sail which first collapsed as he brought the boat close to the wind. It became necessary when giving orders aboard to quickly distinguish between the weather edge of the sail and the lee edge and the name 'luff' was applied to whichever edge was to windward depending on the tack the vessel was sailing on. You may appreciate that the point of collapse of the luff of a squaresail could be delayed by tightly 'bowsing down' (pulling down) the luff of the sail and the lower windward corner came to be known as the tack.

Experience is the best teacher but it sometimes works remarkably slowly. It puzzles me that sailors of the Western world should have taken so long in tumbling to the fact that if, instead of bending their sails to a yard slung across the mast, they bent them instead to a yard whose end was actually pivoting on the mast, and then laced the luff to the mast, they could then brace the yard much farther aft at the free end while keeping the luff bowsed tightly down, and by this means begin to sail not only across, but rather more into the wind.

It must have been at this stage that they began to realise it was the luff of the sail when set in this fashion against the mast, that was driving them to windward, and on this point of sailing the leach was largely useless. It didn't take a stroke of genius therefore to assume that, in order to sail even better to windward the best thing to do was to increase the length of the luff. In the early stages this was done by swinging the yard up from its pivoting point on the mast so that the upper edge of the squaresail, though still at an angle with the mast, began nevertheless to act as an extension of the luff itself.

So for the first time we see the fore-and-aft rig proper where the luff is appreciated as doing nearly all the work in getting the boat up to windward, and the clew was often attached to another lower spar called the boom which also pivoted against the mast at its forward end.

By this time there was developing in the commercial cargo-carrying ships a combination of both square and fore-and-aft sails in one ship. Frequently three or more jibs were set forward on a large spar jutting out over the bow of the ship, called a jibboom or bowsprit. Squaresails were then set on the foremast and mainmast, while another fore-and-aft sail was set on the after mast, called the mizzen mast. This after sail was called the mizzen sail.

This was the style of rig adopted by the famous trading ships which used to make superbly fast passages with a fair degree of versatility regarding the angle they could sail in relation to the wind line. By this time the smaller boats such as fishing smacks and the like were dispensing altogether with the squaresails set on yards across the mast, and setting headsails and

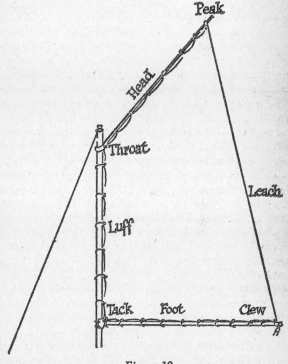

Figure 16

Gaff mainsail. Early form of fore-and-aft sail

fore-and-aft mainsails on a yard which was angled well up from the horizontal: the latter now frequently called a gaff. This came to be known as the gaff rig as illustrated in Figure 16. Note the differences in the names of its parts when compared with the Bermudan sail in Figure 3.

By now it was a recognised fact that the taller the luff of the sail the better would be the windward performance of a boat. To effect this lengthening of the luff a topmast would often be added to extend the normal mast height considerably, and a

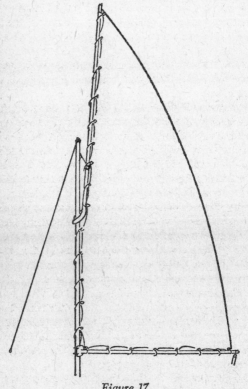

Figure 17

Gunter rig.   A development of the fore-and-aft sail

separate sail called a topsail was set with its peak hoisted to the truck (top) of the topmast, and the foot attached to the gaff. Now you see we have what amounts to what is called a 'high aspect ratio' Bermudan sail. But the method of achieving this was rather clumsy, calling for another mast right up aloft in addition to the gaff up there, which all means weight in the very last place one wishes to have any weight in a boat.

It wasn't long before someone struck upon the idea of dispensing with the topmast altogether and swinging the upper end of the gaff vertically so that the gaff itself formed an extension of the mast, doing away with the topmast. So we now have one mainsail instead of a main and topsail, and this rig became dubbed the 'leg of mutton' sail and later became known as the Gunter rig. (See Figure 17).

We are now really getting close to the modern Bermudan sail which is the most efficient non-rigid aerofoil available for use in a boat.

But efficiency is not the only consideration which must be taken into account when designing the sail plan of a boat. It is easier for a small crew to handle a number of small sails than one or two very large sails, and for this reason boats were rigged often with two masts on which were set Gunter, Gaff, or Bermudan sails and Figure 18 includes various types of two masted vessels which may still be seen.

At the same time as the more efficient sail shapes were evolving, so more efficient hull shapes were evolving along with them. It was recognised that a hull which did everything possible to diminish leeway helped to make the sails more efficient and you will readily see why the short but deep keel became favoured more and more as opposed to the long, straight and fairly shallow keel. When tacking the fore-and-aft rigged boat it's very much easier to swing the hull in the water round a central deep pivot point than it is to swing a long horizontal keel. What is more, within certain limits the deeper the keel penetrates down into the water, the more efficient it becomes with regard to stopping leeway.

You will appreciate that to tack a square rigger was a frightful business, since at some point all the sails had to 'be aback' —blown back and pressed against the mast and spars—as the

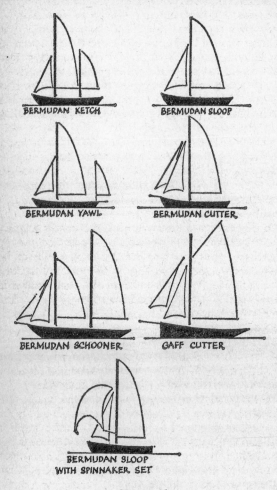

BERMUDAN KETCH   BERMUDAN SLOOP

BERMUDAN YAWL   BERMUDAN CUTTER

BERMUDAN SCHOONER   GAFF CUTTER

BERMUDAN SLOOP
WITH SPINNAKER SET

Figure 18

Types of rigs

vessel swung her head through the eye of the wind. It was a complicated manoeuvre, calling for a lot of searoom in certain ships because it was sometimes necessary for the vessel to be carrying sternway before manipulation of the rudder could effectively swing her head through the wind's eye and persuade her to fill on the opposite tack. For this reason a square rigger would frequently choose to run down wind in order to change tacks, thus maintaining full speed, and this was called 'wearing ship'. In a fore-and-aft rig this would be the equivalent of a gybe. But of course you can't gybe a squaresail any more than you can 'wear ship' in a fore-and-aft rig.

Almost all modern dinghies are either Bermudan or Gunter rig, and whereas the Gunter rig suffers the disadvantage of slightly more weight up aloft combined with a somewhat disturbed airflow, it has the big advantage when ashore of being easier to stow away and trail since the mast is shorter and the gaff can be laid alongside it—often actually inside the boat.

Anyone interested in the evolution of sail shapes and hull designs will find the little book 'Sails through the Centuries' by Sam Svensson (drawings by Gordan Macfie) published by Macmillan quite absorbing, and 'Sailing ships and Sailing Craft' by George Goldsmith-Carter, published by Paul Hamlyn in paperback version is a fascinating colour history of the development of sailing craft.

TIDES

Tides are vertical movements of the water on the face of the earth. Tidal streams are the horizontal movements of the water necessary to allow the vertical rises and fall of the tide.

By far the greatest tide-forming force on earth is the gravitational pull of the moon. Any body with a large mass such as the earth, sun and moon, will have an attractive force which is proportional to the mass of the body, so while it is true to say that most of the tide-forming forces are due to the moon (which is a fairly small heavenly body but very near to the earth), nevertheless we cannot discount the tide-forming effect of the sun which, although it is a tremendous distance away has a huge mass. It therefore has a strong pull on the earth—strong enough to keep the earth in perpetual orbit around it.

It is easy to understand that the sun or the moon, or both together, will tend to pull the seas on the earth's surface into a hump beneath them. This being the case, and bearing in mind that our earth is rotating on its own axis once in twenty-four hours, one might be forgiven for expecting there to be only one High Water (one hump) every twenty-four hours. It would probably be, one might reason, when the sun or moon or both are directly overhead.

Not so simple alas! At any chosen place on the earth's surface (except the Poles) there are as an experienced fact, TWO High Water humps every twenty-four hours. Two High Tides for each single rotation of the earth on its axis—and one occurs almost diametrically opposite the other! It is certainly not what one would expect, but for those who cannot leave a mystery unsolved I'm going to explain why this should be. For those who can just accept facts it won't affect your learning about tides to skip the next eight paragraphs.

The force of gravity between two bodies of a given mass is in inverse proportion to the square of the distance separating them. This is probably all Greek to you but what it means for practical purposes is that the nearer the bodies are to one another, the stronger will be their gravitational attraction.

Before going any further it is necessary to define a word which scientists use rather differently to the manner in which you or I use it. The word is acceleration. To you or me, acceleration simply means 'getting faster'. To the scientist it means any change of velocity. This is not by any means the same thing. When a car speeds up in relation to the ground it is accelerating —the scientist would agree with this—but when it slows down the scientist would also describe it as accelerating, because it is changing its velocity. What's more, when it turns a corner it is also accelerating because it is changing its direction away from a straight line, and therefore changing its velocity in relation to the straight line (which would be its natural and unaffected path if no force were applied to it).

Now think of the earth orbiting in a predictable ellipse round the sun, and held in that orbit by the mutual gravitational effect of both bodies. In so far as the earth is permanently 'turning a corner' (being pulled away from the straight line which would

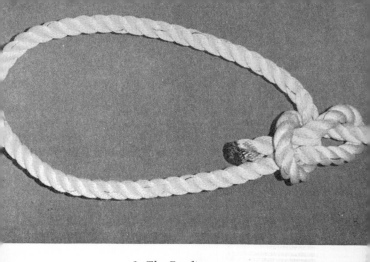

1. The Bowline

2. Fisherman's Bend

3. Sheet-bend

4. Figure-of-eight

6. *Clove hitch*

5. *Reef-knot*

7. *Rolling hitch*

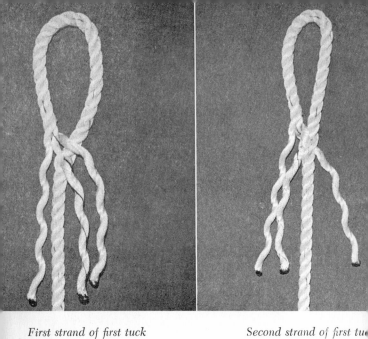

First strand of first tuck

Second strand of first tuck

8. Eyesplice

Third strand of first tuck

First tuck complete

form a tangent to its orbit), the earth may be said to be in a constant state of acceleration toward the sun. This doesn't mean that the earth is falling into the sun—it simply means that it is not proceeding in a straight line which it would follow if the sun's gravity stopped. The sun's gravity is constantly pulling (accelerating) it away from that tangent line, and if you look down the line of acceleration you will be looking directly into the sun.

If we wish to calculate the actual rate of acceleration of earth toward the sun, we would have to take into our calculation the force of gravitational attraction between the two bodies. But this depends on the distance separating them, so we have to ask ourselves: 'which part of the earth's diameter shall we take when feeding in this distance factor to our calculation? Shall we take the distance separating the nearer face of earth to sun or the distance separating the farther face of earth to sun?'

A bit of thought will soon show that neither will be correct; earth must respond to the MEAN of the gravitational pull—a distance exactly halfway between her two faces. This will be from the centre of earth to the sun, because earth is a three dimensional body and so must respond with the mean of her diameter to the sun's pull.

But this is not the case with the seas on earth's surface: these are free to respond independently of the earth beneath them. So what happens is this: the seas on the face nearest to the sun say ... 'this earth on which I'm resting just isn't accelerating (falling toward) the sun fast enough for the gravity which is affecting me. . . . I'm going on ahead!' So it does, to form a High tide hump roughly beneath the sun.

On the opposite face of the earth however, away from the sun, things are very different. The seas here say ... 'this earth on which I'm resting is accelerating toward the sun too fast for the sun's gravity which is affecting me. I'm going to lag behind a bit and respond correctly!' This it does, so forming another High tide hump just about diametrically opposite the first. So one has two High tides on the rotating surface of earth, and not just one as might be expected.

Exactly the same thing applies to the earth-moon system, but in a more appreciable fashion since the moon is so very much nearer earth and therefore the distance separating the two faces of earth from the moon is a proportionally greater fraction of the total distance from earth to moon.

Thinking now of the sun and moon as two huge gravity 'magnets' pulling the seas on earth, it will be evident that when both are at one side of the earth they will be augmenting each

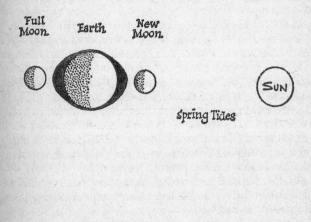

Spring Tides

Neap Tides

Figure 19

Position of sun and moon in relation to earth at Spring and Neap tides

others pull and thus form large tidal humps on opposite sides of the earth. Likewise when they are on diametrically opposite sides of the earth, while they are working against each other in direction of pull, they are nevertheless still augmenting each others 'reciprocal' humps! Thus they again form very High tides.

But when the moon is at right angles to the earth-sun line, moon and sun will be struggling with each other to form their respective humps at different points of earth's surface, and since there is only a limited amount of water on earth it has to try to satisfy both sun and moon, resulting in a large distribution of the High tide area over the earth's face. This means a mediocre sort of High tide hump caused mostly by the moon. This latter is what we experience as Neap tides (low High and high Low), or to put it more clearly, at Neaps there is a small RANGE of tide. When sun and moon are augmenting their respective tidal effects we experience Spring tides (high Highs and low Lows) or a large RANGE of tide. The range of tide therefore is great at Springs and small at Neaps. (See Figure 19).

So the next time you look into the night sky and see either a full or new moon you will know that it must be Spring tides. If you see a half moon, either waxing or waning, it will be Neap tides. (See Figure 20). From the practical point of view it makes a heck of a difference, for if you ignore the state of the tide the chances are you'll have some frustrating sailing. Work with the tides and you will be more likely to go places fast and safely.

You will find the predicted times of High and Low water in Tide Tables which are small books, generally on sale in shops near any port. The Harbourmaster's Office will be almost certain to have a list exhibited. These tables often also give the height of tide in feet above Chart Datum, which is the level below which the depths are given on the chart and above which the height of the tide is measured. This Chart Datum level is selected during the initial survey of an area and may be taken as a height below which the tide at that place very seldom falls. You will note from these tables that the time of High or Low water falls approximately one hour later each day.

A point worth noting: times listed in the Tide Tables may be Greenwich Mean Time which is, of course, one hour earlier

SPRING TIDES

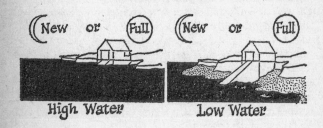

High Water   Low Water

NEAP TIDES

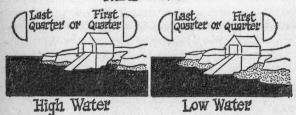

High Water   Low Water

Figure 20

*Quarters of the moon in relation
to Spring and Neap tides*

than our now permanent British Summer Time. But this will
always be noted on the Tide Tables. The following definitions
and Figure 21 will be useful in understanding the tides:

TIDAL DEFINITIONS

MEAN LEVEL is the average level of the surface of the sea.

RANGE OF THE TIDE represents the vertical distance travelled
between one Low water and the succeeding High water.
Spring tides have a large range and Neap tides have a low
range.

TIDAL OSCILLATION A tide wave represents one vertical oscillation either side the mean level of the sea and includes one high water and the succeeding low water.

HIGH WATER AND LOW WATER The highest and lowest level reached by the surface of the sea in one tidal oscillation.

MEAN HIGH WATER NEAPS AND MEAN HIGH WATER SPRINGS are the average heights of high water neaps and high water springs taken over a long period.

CHART DATUM The level below which depths are shown on the chart. The height of the tide at any moment must therefore be added to obtain an actual depth. The tide very seldom falls below Chart Datum.

EQUINOCTIAL SPRING TIDES These occur in March and September when the sun is vertically above our Equator. This being the case, sun, moon and earth all lie in the same plane and the gravitational pull is therefore acting on exactly the same point on the earth's surface, resulting in the greatest range of the tides possible during the year. A boat driven on to a beach at High Water equinoctial tides in September may not be expected to float again until the equinoctial spring tides in the following March. The normal fortnightly spring tides between these equinoxes will not be quite so high unless local weather conditions result in abnormal tides due to strong winds.

THE RISE OF A TIDE is the height of High Water above Chart Datum (see Figure 21).

ON THE BEACH; BE TIDE CONSCIOUS

Two or three times every season I hear a dismal story from some dinghy owner who, on completion of the day's sailing, has put his dinghy ten feet or so up the beach away from the last high water mark. He stowed the anchor and all gear neatly in the boat and went home secure in the knowledge that his boat was snug until the following weekend. He had overlooked the fact that the tides were Neap. Each high tide on successive days crept a little further up the beach until roughly three or four days later the dinghy floated. With an offshore wind it was soon carried out to sea, and what happened then is a matter of luck. Possibly a local fisherman—always on the lookout for this type of incompetence—took the boat in tow and claimed a well deserved fiver for saving the craft from probable total loss. On one occasion a Wayfarer subjected to this sort of thoughtlessness was picked up by a merchant ship many miles south of the Isle of Wight. She discharged it in a foreign port and it was eventually returned to the owner not much the worse for wear, but this was a lucky recovery and the chances are that such a mistake can cost you your dinghy.

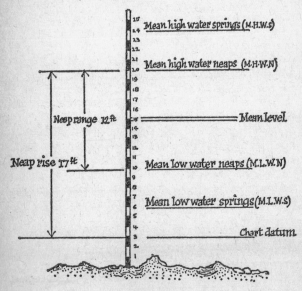

Figure 21

Tidal definitions

When working from a beach be very tide conscious. Always ensure that the boat when finished with is placed well above the highest Spring tideline, and you will be well advised, if you need to leave her for long periods, to come to a financial arrangement with a local boatyard or boatman to keep an eye on her in your absence. Strong winds can easily blow a light dinghy over and may result in a broken mast.

It's wise, if you know the direction of the prevailing wind in the area, to head the dinghy into the wind, and if she is on a sandy beach to bank the sand well up either side the hull to form a wide support in which she sits snugly. The trouble with sand is that when the wind blows round the hull it scours the

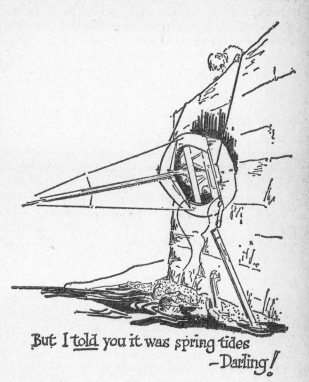

But I told you it was spring tides
— Darling!

sand gradually away, and before long your dinghy may either be capsized into a hole of her own digging, or settled down—self buried as it were—which is all very well for stability but distressing when you see the amount of sand in her cockpit!

It pays to have a boom-up cover. By this I mean a stout canvas overall cover which may be shipped over the top of the boom when the forward end of the boom is housed in the gooseneck and the after end is resting down on the transom. This forms a splendid ridgepole which keeps sand and rain out of the boat, but it does not do the boom much good if left shipped for a very long period.

It is a seamanlike precaution to put an anchor out, even though the boat may by your calculation be above the reach of the highest tide. Tides are funny things and tend to be influenced by local wind direction. I have known a predicted High Water to be a good foot higher than the actual tide—and the reverse! Remember that twelve inches of vertical movement may easily mean twelve feet up a shallow sloping beach. To have an anchor out can mean the difference between losing your dinghy or finding her there when you return. But remember when you put out that anchor that the inboard end of the warp has to be made fast to a cleat or some stout structure in the boat! It is advisable also to bury the anchor well below the surface of the beach to give a good grip and remove the chances of a nasty accident. People are not always looking where they walk, and the sharp fluke of certain types of anchors can cause injury.

USE OF LAUNCHING TROLLEY

If you are operating from a concrete hard or an impacted shingle beach you will undoubtedly choose to launch the boat by means of a launching trolley. This is a very simple axle with wheel at either end, and has a long handle which comes from the axle down either side the hull to curve around her bow. The ideal method of getting the boat on the trolley is to ask a couple of friends to stand, one either side the bow, and lift. You then ease the trolley back centrally along the keel until it's just beyond the pivoting point, taking care to see that the centreboard retaining pin is in position, otherwise the plate will drop down. It is wise to have some form of protective covering round the handles of the trolley where they touch the hull at either side, otherwise the latter will probably be badly scratched when launching.

Many dinghy owners use their road trailers for launching the boat, and indeed the better trailers have sealed bearings to make this possible, but sand and salt water make poor bedfellows with steel no matter how carefully the steel may be protected with paint. Road trailers are expensive, and it's a practice I do not advise.

USE OF BOAT ROLLERS

If working off a soft beach you may find that a launching trolley, even if fitted with broad pneumatic tyres, will sink down to the axle and be harder to pull than the boat alone. The best solution to this sort of soft beach is to use two or three of the large inflatable boat rollers available from ship's chandlers. These are large sausage shaped balloons made of really tough rubber-impregnated canvas or stout plastic and are tested at approximately 500 lbs pressure. The secret is not to inflate them really hard—the boat does that when they are in use by squashing!

With intelligent use one person can easily launch a Wayfarer (weighing approximately 420 lbs all-up) down a long shallow beach to the water. The technique is as follows: swing the stern of the boat towards the water, lift the stern a little and nudge the roller as far under the hull—at right angles to the keel—as you can get it with one foot. It is important that it is central, or slightly on the leeward side if a strong wind is blowing. Put the other rollers in the cockpit otherwise you'll be doing a marathon along the beach if there is any wind! Next go to the stem of the boat, lift and push backwards. This is the hardest bit of the whole launching but provided you lift as well as push, the stern of the boat is tilted down on to the roller which takes a great deal of the weight enabling the boat to slide horizontally over it. Every inch further on to the roller you get the hull, the more weight it takes and the easier it becomes.

As soon as the boat begins to roll easily down the beach on the single roller simply guide it so that it stays centrally on that roller until the stern drops gently down beyond the pivot point. Try to stop it going any further until you have put another roller beneath it, otherwise it will be harder to lift. Once the second roller is underneath, the boat will tend to roll of her own accord but the bow will soon drop down off the first roller and brake the movement. Check that the first roller doesn't immediately blow away. After that one just repeats the procedure by lifting the bow and pushing back on to the newly placed roller under the stern. They say the early Polynesians after a war sortie used the live bodies of their captives to launch their huge canoes, but it was a musical affair and should be avoided on the beach if possible.

You may wonder why I recommend launching the boat stern-first on the rollers. It is just because the flatter section of the stern is more easily supported by the full length of the bag and makes that first lift on to the roller bag very much easier. Do make sure however before commencing that your centre-board retaining pin is in position otherwise the tip of the plate may drop with disastrous results to the roller and your muscles. If you have a slipped disc get your friends or your wife to do it!

The reverse procedure up the beach is about the hardest work there is in sailing a dinghy! On the beach where I sail any person within shrieking distance finds himself press-ganged into assisting at this latter job. Until the moment of collapse it's harder to refuse than it is to help!

SAILING ON TIDAL WATERS IN LIGHT AIRS

When sailing from a beach or mooring in tidal waters always think first of your eventual destination. Nine times out of ten in a dinghy this will be back where you started from, so you must consider the direction of flow of the tide with relation to the wind. For instance if the wind and tide are in the same direction it would be foolish to run off downwind and downtide if you need to get back to the beach fairly soon. You'll have a splendid sail downwind and be amazed at the progress you're making, but on trying to sail back you will probably find that any progress made against the wind will be offset by the tidal stream which will be retarding you. You may well find that far from making progress to windward you are actually losing ground. If this is the case you might as well beach the boat immediately and wait for the tide to turn, for every minute delayed may be a few yards farther from your destination. With the tide behind you of course it will help your beat to windward: but the tide may not turn for some five or so hours!

If the wind is against or across the tidal stream it will be wise

when first leaving the beach or mooring to sail against the tide
so that if the wind should die away completely, at least the tide
will be bringing you back again. Always carry two paddles or
a pair of oars if your dinghy is large enough, in case of such an
eventuality. In an emergency of course you can always use a
bit of the boat's equipment such as rudder, bottom boards or
the boom to paddle or punt the boat gently towards the beach,
but you should have the proper equipment.

SAILING FROM A MOORING IN TIDAL WATERS

Sailing from and picking up a mooring in tidal waters presents an interesting problem. If wind and tide are in the same
direction the procedure will be the same as when sailing from
a non-tidal mooring so far as the tactics of leaving the mooring
are concerned and picking it up again, except that when there
is a tide flowing allowance will have to be made for the fact
that the boat will not range quite so far up head-to-wind on to
the mooring buoy due to the retarding effect of the tide.

But if the wind is blowing in the opposite direction to the
tidal flow it may well be that the boat will be lying stern-to-
wind which makes it difficult to hoist the mainsail, and if you
do try you'll come to grief for she will start sailing immediately.
In these conditions simply hoist your jib, cast off the mooring,
and when you are well clear round up head-to-wind and hoist
the mainsail as quickly as possible.

Should the wind be blowing across the tide the boat may lie
half across the tide and half across the wind. In this case do not
lower the plate until you have actually cast the mooring adrift.
If you lower it while still made fast the boat will swing completely head-to-tide which will be across the wind. That precludes getting the mainsail up. Whether you choose to hoist
the main at the mooring in these circumstances is really a
matter for assessment on the spot. If wind is weak and tide
strong you may wisely decide to get clear of the mooring before
hoisting the main. But if the wind is strong and tidal flow weak
you will manage to get the main up while still made fast. Much
depends on the surrounding water: if this is clear then the
operation is fairly simple but if you have other boats moored in
close proximity in a strong tideway it pays to plan your course

of action very carefully and be sure that you can deal with the situation before casting off.

The tactics in picking up a mooring in tidal waters also depend entirely on the relative direction of wind and tide. As already mentioned, when tide and wind are in the same direction the procedure is virtually the same as when in non-tidal water, but with wind against tide it's generally a sound procedure to luff up well to weather of the mooring and drop the main. Then run down under jib alone against the tide. Your speed relative to the buoy may then be adjusted by simply easing or hardening the jibsheet.

With wind across tide, using a bit of expertise one can usually approach on a reach, stemming the tidal stream. As you approach the buoy you will spill more and more wind from the sails to reduce speed. Immediately your crew has grasped the buoy bring the plate right up and drop the sails as soon as possible making sure they come into the boat and not into the water.

This may all seem a little complicated to a beginner but when you have spent an hour or two getting the feel of the boat you will begin instinctively to relate your movements to that invisible wind line and the run of the tide.

COMING UP TO A JETTY

Look at Figure 22. With the wind as indicated it will obviously be unwise to try to come alongside in any form of sailing craft on the weather side of the jetty: the boat will be blown on to the jetty and sails and boom will foul anything and everything there, resulting in torn sails and a damaged boat.

More advisable to approach from the leeward side and luff-up, but in this case you have to take good care that your speed through the water is calculated exactly right, for you have to stop before your stem clouts the jetty. This isn't always easy, and after you have made fast with a line you will still have to pull the stern of the boat alongside against the pressure of wind, but at least the sails are all blowing out well clear of the jetty.

By far the best manoeuvre would be to come alongside the end of the jetty, where you will be placed nicely alongside

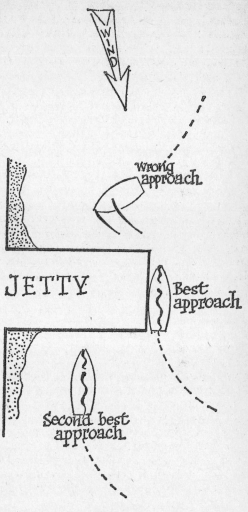

Figure 22

Correct way to approach a jetty

when luffed-up head to wind. What is more, the speed of your approach will not have to be so critical for you have the whole length of the jetty end to accommodate you. The sails will not be fouling anything and you can get them down in peace.

TOWING AND BEING TOWED

Only a very experienced dinghy sailor can manage to tow another boat when he is sailing his own. The point of tow must necessarily come from the transom of the towing boat and this severely limits the manoeuvrability since she is essentially, in all manoeuvres, pivoting round her centreboard. With the transom not free to swing it's very difficult to effect changes of course, and it is possible for the towed boat to range ahead and swing the stern of the boat towing so that she becomes uncontrollable and may well capsize. Don't try it until you feel you really know all the answers, and then expect catastrophe and boast about it for weeks afterwards if it comes off!

If you find yourself in the position of having to accept a tow, always bring the towline in through the fairlead at your stem-head and make sure that you can cast off easily and quickly at the inboard end of the towline even while it is under strain. This is vital for things can happen in your boat which make it imperative that you cease being towed at once. The matter is then in your own hands and you don't have to rely on the towing boat appreciating your need. It is wise also for the chap in the towing boat to be able to likewise cast off the tow while under strain since conditions can be reversed.

Should you be landed in a situation where the wind has died away completely, or perhaps due to breakage of equipment you have to tow the boat yourself, it's useful to remember that you may walk along the beach dry-shod by making the towline fast to some point about a quarter way back along the hull. By doing this, as soon as the strain comes on the towline she will angle away from the beach and tow in deep water whereas if towed by the stem she will constantly sheer back to the beach.

KNOTS AND CORDAGE

The days of natural fibres in rope are almost over. Sisal, hemp or manilla are rarely used for halyards or sheets now and in their place has come the stronger and more flexible synthetic ropes made from terylene and nylon etc. One of the faults of a natural fibre rope is the fact that when wetted it tends to become very stiff and easily kinked which makes it difficult to reeve through blocks or fairleads. Modern multiplait terylene cordage is a great improvement because it will not absorb water and remains as flexible when wet as when dry. Unlike the three-stranded cordage it also does not kink so easily and is therefore ideal for halyards and sheets where it is essential that nothing fouls up.

Rope and wire is measured by its circumference. A ⅜" circumference wire will be approximately ⅛" in diameter. Most dinghy sheets are of multiplait terylene 1¼" in circumference and the only disadvantage of this multiplait braided rope is the difficulty of splicing. In fact it's just 'not on' to attempt to splice it, and to make an eye in such a rope one must fray out (unlay) about four inches of the end and wrap the separated strands evenly back round the laid rope forming an eye of the required size. This has then to be tightly whipped over with twine. It makes a neat eye, but takes longer that the normal eyesplice to do.

The trouble about learning to tie knots is that, like most things, unless one has constant need to use them one very soon forgets how to tie them. The test of a good knot is that it should do its job without any chance of failing yet, no matter what strain has been put on it, it will be easy to untie.

A knot which is impossible to cast quickly off is a danger in a boat, and all the knots illustrated in the accompanying photographs have stood the test of time in this respect.

THE BOWLINE Photo 1. Used to form a loop in the end of a rope. The ability to form a quick loop, or 'bight', comes in useful on many occasions—such as making fast a berthing warp over a bollard on a jetty. It is what one should use to secure a line round oneself if in the water since one can be hauled up a ship's side thereby without fear of being crushed due to the knot slipping. It's worth practising tying the bowline round oneself beneath the armpits until it becomes quite automatic.

FISHERMAN'S BEND Photo 2. A useful knot for securing any rope to a ringbolt or post such as may be found on a jetty, or to the ring of an anchor.

SHEET BEND Photo 3. For joining two ropes of unequal size. The 'bight' is formed in the thicker of the two ropes and the thinner end is worked around the 'bight' as shown.

FIGURE OF EIGHT Photo 4. This is a stopper knot put in the end of a rope to prevent it passing through a sheetbend or block. Easy to untie even when the rope is wet.

REEF KNOT Photo 5. Perhaps the most frequently used of all knots. For joining two ropes of equal size.

CLOVE HITCH Photo 6. Used for fastening a rope to a spar or rail, but it must be used with caution for if the spar can rotate the hitch will roll until it pulls completely off. If the spar is rigid however this hitch does not slip easily.

ROLLING HITCH Photo 7. A useful hitch for making a small rope fast to a larger one, or to a spar. Direction of pull must always be as shown otherwise it is possible for it to slip.

EYESPLICE Photo 8. Used for making a permanent eye in the end of a three-stranded rope. Approximately nine inches of the rope end is unlaid into its three separate strands. I always form the eye in my left hand so that it is looking toward my left, then drop one of the three separated strands down either side of the laid rope leaving the third on top. The lay immediately beneath the single strand on top is now prised open and the top strand passed away from one through the hole so formed and pulled neatly down into the rope. The eye is then given a half twist and one of the remaining single strands is placed over and under the lay of the rope immediately beneath it. The last strand is the most tricky. You will see that the two previous strands are now emerging from gaps which are adjacent to each other and there is only one gap from which a strand is not yet coming at the same level. The third strand must be brought forward toward you and then pushed through the lay in a direction away from one so that it emerges from the only remaining gap at the same level as the other two strands. This completes the first tuck and you can check that it is correct by simply holding up the rope and seeing that all three strands are emerging 120 degrees apart from each other at the same level. From then on it's simple: each strand continues to go over and under the one beneath it and next to it. For natural fibres such as sisal, hemp and manilla a minimum of three tucks should be used. But for three stranded terylene or nylon which has very much less friction a minimum of five tucks should be taken.

THE COMMON WHIPPING

This is for preventing the end of a rope unlaying and is shown in detail in Figure 23. Place the end of the whipping twine along the rope as shown and pass the turns of twine tightly round the rope trapping the end firmly beneath the turns. Turn the twine against the lay of the rope and work toward the rope's end. After about a quarter of an inch of whipping lay the other end of the twine along the rope and pass the remaining turns over it taking the loop of twine over the end of the rope with each turn. When you have run out of loop, pull this second end of the twine through the turns you have passed over it until taut, which completes the last turn round the rope. Cut off both loose ends.

It is worth remembering that when opening a new coil of three-stranded rope the coil should be stood on the end allowing the rope to be taken off anti-clockwise from the centre. Otherwise, if taken from the outside of the coil a confusion of kinks will result.

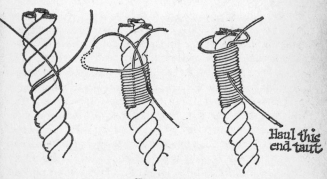

Haul this end taut

Figure 23
The common whipping

4

Safety Afloat

It is common sense to take precautions against accidents and the most obvious accident which presents itself to a beginner in a boat is the risk of drowning. By comparison with road accidents this is rare indeed but this is not to say that one should ever adopt the attitude 'it won't happen to me!'

Physical injury to a beginner is far more likely since he will not be familiar with the movements of the boat nor be familiar with the position of the boat's component parts and fittings. Unless his reactions are very quick he can easily be struck a severe blow by the boom, and when moving to compensate the rocking of the boat he may well graze his shins or clout his toes. However, after an hour or two in the dinghy these hazards will begin to lessen because his reactions and judgement will have become almost automatic.

Always wear some form of lifejacket before going afloat. Broadly speaking these come in two forms. One will keep you afloat even when unconscious in a manner whereby you can continue to breathe. It does this by rolling you on to your back and supporting the back of the head on a cushion of buoyancy. The other type—commonly known as 'personal buoyancy' as opposed to the lifejacket proper—is in the form of a waistcoat which generally laces down the front. This keeps one buoyant, but if unconscious it allows the nose to drop beneath the water. Nevertheless it is favoured by most dinghy sailors because of its simplicity and because it allows great freedom of movement in the boat. I would advise that non-swimmers and young children should wear a proper lifejacket, whereas competent swimmers, may favour the personal buoyancy waistcoat.

As already remarked, it is worth remembering even if you are a strong swimmer that wearing any form of buoyancy will tend to hamper your ability to swim. This is particularly relevant if, after capsizing, you see some part of the boat's equipment floating away and decide to go after it. You may well discover that the equipment—and the boat—are blowing away from you faster than you can swim.

We have already considered in Chapter 1 the merits of buoyancy in the boat herself, either built-in or tied in, and you may remember that the principle of more and more buoyancy for more and more safety is not altogether sound, since the higher a boat floats out of the water when she is capsized the faster she'll blow away from you if you become separated from her.

It is a wise precaution on a calm day to go out in your boat or the boat you are going to crew and deliberately exercise capsize drill. You will soon learn the best method with any particular class of dinghy to effect the righting of the boat, as already discussed in chapters 1 and 2.

SAFETY EQUIPMENT

Always ensure that your rigging—both standing and running —is in good condition. As a general guide, if ever you find yourself posing the question 'I wonder if that will last this season out!'—replace it. You ought to feel sure that every item of the hull and equipment is sound, and it is money well spent to see that it remains so.

Equipment which would normally come under the heading of safety in a dinghy would include a small anchor and about 60 feet of approximately ⅝" circumference terylene anchor warp. To anchor safely one should in theory lay out about three times the depth of water by way of anchor warp. Of course this is not always possible, but it is a good guide because the less warp you lay out the more chance you have of dragging anchor.

One, or perhaps a pair of canoe paddles should be carried, or in a larger dinghy a pair of oars and crutches (rowlocks). If sailing off a sea shore, or in any circumstances where it would be possible on being disabled to drift out to sea, you should also carry a daylight distress signal. These may be purchased from any ship's chandler and take the form of a small cylinder which, when ripped open at the top, gives off a cloud of brilliant orange smoke. You may feel a bit of a fool if ever you let it off, but at least you'll be sure that plenty of people know you need assistance.

A plastic bucket should form a part of every well equipped dinghy. After a capsize you can sluice a tremendous amount of water out of the cockpit with it.

Everything must, of course, be secured in the boat otherwise you'll find yourself exclaiming, 'But I HAD a splendidly equipped boat before it happened!'

It is wise to develop a form of cockpit check prior to launching the boat. I do this, and it goes as follows:

1 Rigging screws—are the lock nuts done up tightly so as to prevent the barrel unscrewing?
2 Are the split pins in position at both ends of the rigging screws?
3 Anchor and warp aboard and secured?
4 Plastic bucket aboard and secured?
5 If buoyancy bags fitted are they all properly inflated and fastened in the boat?
6 If built-in buoyancy, are the hatches properly fastened?
7 Rudder hangings: any sign of looseness due to screws pulling out or bolts shearing?

HELPING OTHERS IN TROUBLE

Inevitably the occasion will arise sooner or later when you find yourself going to the assistance of another chap who has capsized and due either to inexperience or unfitness is not able to get the boat righted, or perhaps even to climb back aboard. After a few efforts he will be rather exhausted and probably just holding on to the capsized boat waiting for help to arrive. The first thing to remember is that it is unwise to attempt to come alongside the actual boat: you will probably damage your own craft, or the other, and more important probably injure the chap you are trying to help by crushing him between the two boats. I always adopt the following procedure:

(a) Sail slowly past just to leeward clear of the boat, and ask if he can swim. If he replies that he can, I tell him that I shall return and luff head-to-wind very near his capsized boat so that he can swim the few feet to me and be pulled aboard over my transom.

(b) If he cannot, or if he is in any state that indicates it were better for him not to leave the capsized boat even for the few feet he has to come to me, I tell him that I shall return and luff up to leeward and pass him a line which he should attach to the capsized boat. Once this is done it is an easy matter to pull one's dinghy gently up to within a few inches of the other boat without hitting it, and help the chap back to the transom of your own boat and aboard. This way you will continue to lie head-to-wind as long as you need without actually risking touching the other boat which simply acts as a drogue, or sea-anchor, in the water.

(c) If the chap just isn't capable of helping, or doesn't appear to have his wits about him sufficiently to co-operate then there is nothing for it: you will have to luff gently up on to the other boat from the leeward side, taking good care that your centreboard doesn't become foul of any bits of her rigging etc. in the water. If you have a crew get him to hold on to the other boat without actually allowing your own boat to strike it: easier said than done in a choppy sea. If he can grasp a trailing sheet or something similar, so much the better. Then throw the victim a line and see that he has it secure round himself before attempting to tow him to you and back to your transom.

Never attempt to tow a waterlogged boat ashore with your sailing dinghy. It will almost certainly result in another capsize. Call in the assistance of a power boat and hope that the driver will have the common sense to approach the hull on the side opposite the mast, making his towline fast to the bow of the towed boat before towing VERY GENTLY to the nearest safe shore. I have seen more damage done by a well intentioned tow than would have resulted if the boat had been allowed to drift alone to the shore!

MAN OVERBOARD

In the unlikely event of your crew falling over the side, I would strongly discourage an immediate gybe in order to sail round and luff up on to him. Psychologically you'll probably be in a bit of a tizzy at seeing your crew disappear with a splosh, and since this is most likely to happen in a brisk wind when the boat is moving quickly, you may well find yourself in the water as well if you attempt to gybe to get back to him.

You will appreciate that it is imperative that you do approach him in the water luffed up so that the power is switched off—if you try to pick him up while still sailing you will probably break his neck, dislocate his shoulder, or run him down completely and probably capsize yourself in the process.

The method I always adopt and teach is to immediately put the boat on to a beam reach straight across the wind after he has gone overboard. I then sail away from him for five or six boat's lengths with the jib free, and tack. Immediately after the tack I ease mainsheet and keep the helm up so that she runs back on a broad reach across her original track, getting down wind of the man in the water. After that it is just a case of luffing up so as to bring him slightly on the weather side of the boat. That way he will not be drifted under the hull due to the boat making leeway over the top of him. Remember that a chap in the water who is losing interest can very easily go under the hull and wrap himself round the centreboard. But that is looking on the black side of things, and more often than not the crew will only be weak from laughter!

Remember to get him aboard over the transom, and never take your eyes off him once he has gone overboard for it's all too easy to lose contact with a head in the water particularly if it is sunward of you. This performing of a figure-of-eight to pick up a man overboard will take a few seconds longer than gybing round, but it gives you time to think and nobody is going to drown in the twenty seconds or so it takes to get back to your crew who will be wearing a buoyancy aid anyway.

ARTIFICIAL RESPIRATION

In the event of your having to render artificial respiration bear in mind from the start one all-important fact. If the victim is not obviously breathing then it's imperative that air be got into his lungs immediately. The 'kiss of life' is now accepted as being the most efficient method. If the chap is already ashore lie him on his back with something behind his shoulders so that the head falls back. Open the mouth and check that nothing is obviously blocking the throat such as seaweed or the tongue, which must be pulled forward. Close his nostrils with one hand, exhale deeply, take a fairly deep breath and place your mouth over his. Exhale and check as you do so that his chest rises. Do this from ten to fifteen times a minute—faster for infants, and be careful not to blow too hard with small children because their lungs are not so capacious or tough.

DON'T GIVE UP. Continue until a Doctor arrives. Minutes— almost literally seconds can make the difference between re- covery and death or permanent brain damage. If the casualty has apparently ceased breathing while still in the water you should try to effect the kiss of life there and then though this may mean going into the water with him. Not easy, but neces- sary. Keep calm and get on with whatever is needed to start him breathing again.

SAILING IN NEW WATERS

Always check before launching in new waters—especially if these are tidal—on local dangers. There may be a bar across the entrance to an estuary, or a particularly strong tidal flow over rocks etc. A few sensible precautions can often avoid unneces- sary damage or hazard, and the local harbourmaster or sailing club will be only too willing to advise. Sometimes there are restricted areas set aside for sailing and water-skiing. On some reservoirs sailing is strictly forbidden, and on others certain precautions have to be taken with regard to hull disinfection before launching.

RULES OF THE ROAD AND COURTESY AFLOAT

The authorities have been wise in recognising the completely different manoeuvring and handling characteristics of power boats and sailing boats.

It is obvious that a sailing boat which is governed completely by the wind cannot always manoeuvre with the ease of a power driven craft, and the latter is therefore generally required to give way to sailing craft.

A ship however, when negotiating a narrow channel could hardly be expected to alter course and thereby possibly hazard her own safety and all aboard for a small yacht or sailing dinghy. So the basic rule that 'power gives way to sail' has recently been modified to take this into account, and under these circumstances the ship would have the right of way.

What constitutes a 'ship', 'power boat' and a 'narrow channel' may give rise to interesting discussion but the purpose of these rules is to effect safety at sea and only a fool would, in a case of doubt, choose to endanger himself or the other party by deliberately persisting against a commonsense course of safety.

The first sentence of Rule 1(a) of the International Regulations for preventing Collisions at Sea states that the rules shall be followed by all vessels on all waters navigable by seagoing vessels. It includes you.

Rule 17, which deals with sailing craft approaching one another states that when on opposite tacks the craft on port tack shall keep clear, but when the two craft are on the same tack it is the boat to windward which shall keep clear.

Rule 18 deals with power driven craft. When two power driven craft are meeting end on, or nearly end on, each alters course to starboard.

Rule 19 states that when two power driven craft are crossing, the vessel which has the other on her starboard side shall keep out of the way, and superimposed on all these rules is Rule 24 which states that in all circumstances the overtaking vessel keeps clear.

So much for power meeting power and sail meeting sail. Rule 20 starts by saying that a power driven vessel must give way to a sailing craft, but immediately qualifies this in several ways. As already remarked, a sailing boat does not have the right to hamper a power driven craft in a narrow channel and this is further emphasised by rule 25(c) which states that a small power driven boat does not have the right to hamper a large one. These Rules are very sound, and have recently been revised to cater for modern situations as opposed to the old days of square-riggers.

Commonsense precautions when taking avoiding action under the Regulations are dealt with in Rule 22; do not attempt to cross ahead of a Right-of-way vessel, and Rule 23; slacken speed, stop, or go astern.

An overriding condition applicable to all the Rules however states that ... 'in obeying and construing these Rules, due regard shall be had to all dangers of navigation and collision and any special circumstances, including the limitations of the craft involved, which may render a departure from the above Rules necessary in order to avoid imminent (or immediate) danger.'

So you see, if you are in a twelve foot sailing dinghy and a deep draught yacht is approaching in circumstances where you have the right of way you must give due regard to his difficulties, and even though you may have the right of way it would be courteous to keep clear BUT TAKE ACTION WELL IN ADVANCE because the other craft will be well aware that you have the right of way and may be preparing to take avoiding action even at a slight risk to himself. In this circumstance unless your own avoiding action is taken in good time it could be that you both act simultaneously, resulting in a collision or a state of blood pressure.

There is nothing more discourteous than for a small boat to proceed in such a manner that she causes concern to a large vessel. Put yourself in the position of the Captain of a ship navigating thousands of tons down a narrow channel and having to wonder whether a gaggle of dinghies half a mile ahead are, or are not, going to get out of his way. GET OUT OF THE WAY and STAY OUT OF THE WAY until the ship has passed.

BUOYAGE SYSTEM

As you already know, the tidal stream caused by a rising tide is referred to as the 'flood', whereas the tidal stream caused by a falling tide is referred to as the 'ebb'. The flood tide will, of course, always flow into an estuary since it has to do so to fill the estuary up, but out at sea it is necessary to know the direction in which the flood and ebb streams flow. This is particularly important because it is to the direction in which the flood stream flows that the buoyage system is related.

The rules state that when proceeding in that direction in

which the flood stream shall flow, a can shaped buoy must be left on the port hand. Such a buoy is known as a port hand buoy, and when entering an estuary you therefore proceed to starboard of it, leaving it on your port hand. It follows that when leaving the estuary (i.e. going against the flood stream) one leaves it on the Starboard hand and goes to port of it.

A conical buoy (converging to a point at the top) must be left on the starboard hand when entering an estuary or harbour. One proceeds to port of it. When leaving harbour of course the reverse applies.

A spherical buoy indicates that the channel divides and one may pass on either side, but if one channel is more easily navigable than the other this is indicated by the colour of the buoy (see Figure 24). Spherical buoys are called middle ground buoys and are coloured in horizontal alternate bands.

Port hand buoys are painted red, or red and white chequers.

Starboard hand buoys are painted black, or black and white chequers.

Middle ground buoys may be painted red and white horizontal stripes or black and white horizontal stripes. The former indicates that when entering harbour the main channel is to starboard, or that both channels are equally navigable. The latter indicates that when entering harbour the main channel is to port. You see the colours are the same as port and starboard hand buoys respectively, though the shape and pattern are different. Figure 24 shows the three main types of channel buoys.

It is advisable to understand this buoyage system although the channel buoys are more for the guidance of larger vessels, nevertheless if you're sailing a dinghy in unfamiliar waters it will pay you to keep to the channels unless you know the area well. In this respect it is worth while taking a good look at the water at low tide to make a mental note of any exposed dangers which will not be visible at high tide.

Buoys marking wrecks are always painted green, but their shapes have exactly the same significance as normal channel buoys.

At night the major channel buoys are lit, port hand buoys having either one to four red flashes, or two, four, or six white flashes. Starboard hand buoys are lit with either one, three, or

Port hand Buoy
(Red, or Red & White chequered.)

Starboard hand Buoy
(Black, or Black & White chequered)

Middle ground Buoy
Red & White, or Black & White Horizontal stripes

Figure 24

Channel buoys

116

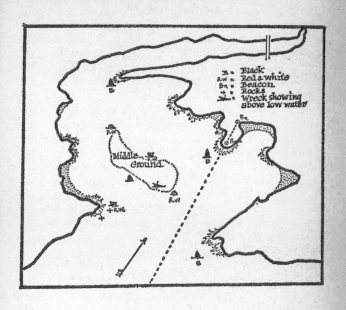

Figure 25

Chart of an imaginary estuary

five white flashes. Wreck buoys carry green flashing lights: port hand two flashes, starboard hand three flashes, and either hand one flash.

The light characteristics of buoys are given on the chart of the area, and it is by this means that identification of the exact buoy is made at night. Figure 25 shows an imaginary estuary illustrating the buoys as they would be positioned relative to the channels.

In the upper reaches of shallow estuaries one often meets with local navigational aids such as poles with topmarks, stuck in the mud. But you'll generally find that the topmarks conform to the main system. Navigation proper is really outside the requirements of the dinghy sailor, and although I often ship a compass just beneath the tiller in my Wayfarer it is not really possible to use it for taking accurate 'fixes' showing my position on a chart. I use it simply as a rough guide in the event of fog coming down. Unless you are a very experienced sailor you ought never to be at sea in a dinghy under circumstances where navigation in the true sense of the word is necessary.

SOUND SIGNALS

These are audible signals which a vessel makes to indicate changes of direction at sea and are given on the siren of a large ship, or on the foghorn or hooter of a small boat. (See Figure 26).

ONE BLAST: I am directing my course to starboard.

TWO BLASTS: I am directing my course to port.

THREE BLASTS: My engines are going astern. Note that this does not necessarily mean that the vessel herself is going astern—she may be carrying considerable headway even though her engines are in reverse.

VISUAL SIGNALS

These take the form of 'shapes' which are hoisted in a prominent position on board a ship or on land adjacent to a coastguard station etc. (See Figure 27).

ON BOARD SHIP: One black ball hoisted aloft: I am at anchor.
Two black balls hoisted aloft vertically above one another: I am not under command.

I am directing my course to Starboard

Hoot Hoot

I am directing my course to Port

My engines are going Astern.

Figure 26

Sound signals

I am anchored

I am not under command

I am aground

Figure 27,

Visual Signals

Three black balls hoisted aloft vertically above one another: I am aground.

Note: The term 'not under command' means simply that the vessel is manoeuvring with difficulty. She does not necessarily need assistance, but merely wishes to warn all concerned that she may not manoeuvre as one might expect.

ASHORE: Black cone, point uppermost: Northerly gale imminent.

Black cone, point downward: Southerly gale imminent.

DISTRESS

In a small boat such as a dinghy the recognised signal to indicate that assistance is required is a slow raising and lowering of the arms sideways, from one's sides to vertically above the head. The emphasis is on *slowly*.

CLIMATE AND WEATHER

Anyone living in the British Isles will be familiar with such phrases as 'areas of high pressure', 'areas of low pressure', 'depressions', isobars and fronts, all of which are terms used by the Meteorological Office in forecasting weather.

By common usage they come to have a certain amount of significance even to the least knowledgeable of us: one comes to associate good weather with an area of high pressure and most of us, on looking at the barometer, express delight when it has risen. But we do take a great deal for granted and while I do not propose in this book to give a detailed instruction course on how to forecast weather, I do think that a sound knowledge of the basic principles is not only interesting in its own right but also allows one more fully to understand results following on certain atmospheric conditions.

Broadly, the general atmospheric conditions over the whole surface of the earth are referred to as the earth's climate. Localised disturbances in these overall conditions are referred to as weather. The climatic conditions over the earth as a whole follow a fairly uniform pattern due to phenomena known as convection and rotation.

Convection is the name given to what happens when gas such as our atmosphere is heated locally, thereby expanding and becoming relatively lighter which makes it rise up vertically to allow the cooler and heavier surrounding gas to flow in to the space vacated.

If you imagine the earth to be a globe with a mantle of gas covering it fairly uniformly—our atmosphere—and visualise the sun to be a source of heat at one side of the earth, you will readily see that a point on the earth's surface immediately beneath the sun (it will necessarily be in the region of the equator) will receive far more heat than a point near either Pole. This is not because the equator is nearer to the sun than the Poles (the radius of the earth is quite insignificant when compared with the 95 odd million miles separating us from the sun). It is simply due to the fact that at the equator any given area is receiving more rays of heat than is the same area of land at the Poles. Figure 28 will illustrate this.

So we have unequal heating at equator and poles and if we imagine for a moment that the earth were not rotating on its

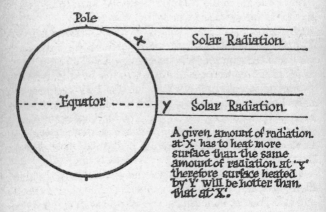

Figure 28

Why the equator is hotter than the poles

own axis, one would expect the gas of our atmosphere to rise upward at the equator thus allowing the surface gas to flow in toward the equator from the cooler North and South Poles. In so doing, the cooler gas will have left a space in the Polar regions, and the gas which has risen will tend to flow at high level toward the Poles so as to fill in this space, cooling as they do so, to sink at the Poles and commence flowing at surface level back towards the equator. There it again heats up, rises, flows at high level back to Polar regions and forms a system of airstreams flowing at surface level from Poles to equator and from equator to Poles at high level. Figure 29 will illustrate this very simplified convectional system.

Our earth however is rotating on its own axis once in twenty-four hours and that axis line is more or less at right angles to a line from earth to sun, depending on the season. It doesn't vary from a right-angle at any time more than twenty-three and a half degrees of arc. At midsummer England is tilted towards the sun and at midwinter we are tilted away from the sun.

So the convectional system just described takes place on the rotating globe and this results in a rather odd phenomena: the high airstream flowing from equator to Pole is deflected to the right of its path in the Northern hemisphere and to the left of its path in the Southern hemisphere.

If you think about this, it's easy to see why. A point on the equator in its rotation round the axis of the earth is travelling some 21,600 nautical miles in twenty-four hours: it's as far away as it can be from the axis line and therefore has a long way to go for one complete rotation. Up near the Poles—let's say ten miles from the actual Pole—a point will only have to travel a short distance to complete one rotation (in this example about thirty miles). Of course the angular distance (360 degrees) will be the same, but the linear distance will be very different from that at the equator.

But the gas which is rising at the equator and flowing toward the Poles is moving round the axis with the equatorial velocity and as it flows at high level toward the poles its own momentum will tend to maintain that velocity. So it appears to over-shoot the ever more slowly moving surface beneath as it travels polewards—to the right of its path in the Northern hemisphere

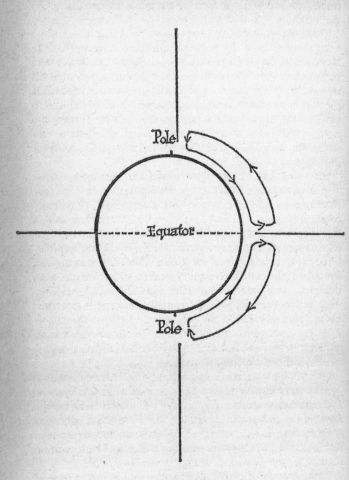

Figure 29
Airflow between poles and equator

and to the left of its path in the Southern hemisphere, since the earth is rotating from West to East.

Similarly, when the cold heavy polar air which is in contact with the surface of the earth and therefore subjected to frictional resistance begins to move toward the equator, it will tend to be carrying with it the slower polar rotation speed and as it moves toward the equator it will pass over a surface which is moving in an ever faster Easterly direction. It will therefore tend to lag behind and appear to again swing toward the right of its path—the West—in Northern hemisphere, and toward the left of its path—the West again—in the Southern hemisphere.

The circulation of air as described from equator to pole at high level and pole to equator at surface level is a tremendous oversimplification, but it should be evident now that due to the rotation of the earth air cannot flow in a straight line from a high pressure area to a low pressure area, and if you think carefully about this you will understand that air moving from a localised high pressure area in the Northern hemisphere, simply because it will have an outward moving direction, must twist in a clockwise fashion when viewed from above. Conversely, air moving in toward a localised low pressure area must twist in an anticlockwise direction because it is moving inwards to a centre when viewed from above. The former (clockwise) motion is called an anticyclone, while the latter (anticlockwise) motion is called a cyclone.

In the Southern hemisphere of course the situation is reversed.

An area of low barometric pressure, conducive to a cyclone, is referred to as a depression or 'low' and you will now see the truth in the well known statement that if you stand with your back to the wind the centre of a depression will lie on your left hand side, whereas the centre of a localised high pressure area, or 'high' will lie on your right hand side.

Looking again at Figure 29, you will realise that the general convectional current there illustrated falls into a slightly more complex pattern on this rotating globe. Cooled air flowing from the north pole Southward toward the equator is diverted to the right of its path from due South through South-West to West. It steadies up on a Westerly path about halfway down to the equator, and since this is cool air from the polar high pressure region it cannot move still further to the right otherwise it would be travelling back Northward to its own high pressure region from which it is escaping.

Similarly the hot air, rising from the equatorial low pressure region is being deflected to its right—in an Easterly direction—until in roughly the same region halfway up to the Pole it is travelling due East. Likewise this high level air cannot swing still more to the right because then it would be moving back to its own low pressure region.

So roughly halfway between equator and pole there is an accumulation of air which may be thought of as a belt of relatively high pressure encircling the earth. This area is known as the Horse Latitudes and exists over the Atlantic, Pacific, and South Indian Oceans, characterised by calm variable winds. The well known Easterly Trade winds lie on the equatorial sides of these belts of high pressure.

Now look at Figure 30. We have areas of high pressure at the poles, low pressure at the equator, and high pressure roughly midway between the two. It follows there has to be an area of relatively low pressure between the polar 'high' and the Horse Latitude 'High'. These low pressure areas do exist and they are referred to as the temperate Belts. The British Isles lie in the Northern one.

We now have the pressure areas depicted in Figure 30 and since high pressure air must flow towards low pressure areas, it is clear (bearing in mind the deflection caused by the earth's rotation) that Horse Latitude 'high' belt will result in North-Easterly (Trade) winds at its equatorial side in the Northern hemisphere, and South-Westerly winds at its Polar side in the Northern hemisphere.

So the Temperate Belt in which the British Isles lie will tend to constantly experience South Westerly winds in its Southern region. To the North of this Temperate Belt however, the flow from the Polar 'high' will give North Easterly winds. So the two different airstreams meet in this Temperate Belt and cause local disturbances in the overall climatic conditions which are called 'weather'. In fact, the climate in the British Isles is nearly all 'weather'!

This cold dense air coming South from the Polar high pressure region is influenced by the sea or by the land. That which originates over the North Atlantic is known as the MARITIME POLAR AIRSTREAM, and while initially it is cold and dry it warms up a bit and absorbs moisture as it travels Southward over the sea whose temperature at the surface is steadily rising as the wind travels farther South.

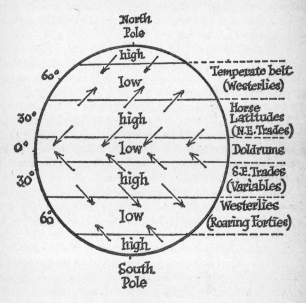

Figure 30

Climatic zones

The Southward travelling airstream which originates over the land masses of Scandinavia and Russia is known as the CONTINENTAL POLAR AIRSTREAM. Unlike water—which tends to heat up slowly and give up its heat slowly—dry land heats up quickly and gives up its heat quickly. So in winter this Continental Polar airstream is cold and dry while in summer it is warm and dry.

To the South of the Temperate Belt the Northward flowing airstream is therefore warm and moist. This is known as the MARITIME TROPICAL AIRSTREAM.

Where, however, these sub-tropical winds moving Northwards originate over the Continental land masses they tend to be very hot and very dry and are known as the CONTINENTAL TROPICAL AIRSTREAM, although after passing over a warm ocean they will have picked up a lot of moisture.

Remember that hot air can hold more water vapour than cold air.

In this Temperate Belt therefore we have in very general terms a cold North Easterly polar airstream in its Northern area and a warm South Westerly airstream from the sub-tropical regions in its Southern area.

These two airstreams do not readily mix but try to flow along each other's face at what is called the POLAR FRONT. During the summer, due to the tilt of the earth on its axis this Polar Front lies roughly between Latitude 45 and 60 degrees North, and in winter between 30 and 50 degrees North because the earth is tilted the opposite way.

But this Front does not remain a straightforward vertical wall of one airstream flowing along another. What happens is that the heavier cold polar airstream undercuts the light warm sub-tropical air, nudging it up and out of its way so to speak and forming what may be thought of as a huge scarf joint in air. Although, as already stated, the two airstreams tend to remain separate, mixing must occur at this scarf joint because the two air masses, by contact with each other, acquire each others characteristics. It does not remain a straight line either, this scarf-jointed Polar Front. Sooner or later a kink forms and a bulge of South Westerly sub-tropical air pushes up North of the normal Front line.

Immediately this happens a fairly predictable pattern of future events may be forecast. The bulge as a whole begins to move East-North-East up the Front and the Western edge of the bulge (cold polar air) swings down and toward the South East continuing to undercut the warm sub-tropical air as it does so. On the advancing Eastern edge of the bulge however the warm sub-tropical air is rather ineffectual in pressing the

128

heavier polar air out of its way, and rather tends to flow in a very gradual incline up over the dense cold air. So the scarf joint on the Eastern edge elongates, and as the bulge (or wedge as it is now becoming) deepens, the western edge tends to catch up the less vigorous Eastern edge.

A narrowing wedge results, the Northern apex of which is going to be the centre of a quite violent convectional disturbance. This must be so, because up there we have a narrow lower pressure hot air mass closely hedged in by a dense cold air mass on either side.

The result is that the hot air escapes upwards and the cold air whips in to fill the space. In so doing the cold air is deflected in an anti-clockwise direction and we have a cyclone, or depression, on our hands. These accursed things are constantly forming along the line of the Polar Front and England lies right in their path.

To be able to speak of depressions or their opposite—'highs' —in anything but the most general relative terms one must create definite units of measurement. Meteorologists use units called millibars to measure pressure in the atmosphere, and one millibar is equal to a pressure of one thousand Dynes per square centimetre. This, I'll guess, means absolutely nothing to you, nor does it to me and it matters not. It's just that one Dyne is the name given to the fundamental Metric Unit of force.

What does begin to have meaning is the fact that the average atmospheric pressure in our Temperate Belt is around 1013 millibars, and this is where the needle of our aneroid barometer (or the level of mercury in a mercury barometer) would rest under these conditions. So when we learn that the centre (up in the apex of that wedge) of a deep depression may experience 970 millibars pressure and conversely that the centre of a good 'high' is reading around 1040 millibars, the whole picture of relative atmospheric pressure begins to have real meaning. The whole span of pressure from a deep 'low' to an intense 'high' comes within about 70 millibars.

On a chart, lines of equal pressure are called isobars, and on weather charts these look very like the contour lines of height on a land map. So you will realise that it makes sense to expect strong winds when the isobars are close together since it means there is a big difference of pressure in a small area. The result is a violent convectional disturbance with associated wind reactions.

On the weather chart the advancing side of a cold front—the Western edge of the wedge—is indicated by a black triangle on the advancing edge of the Front. The advancing edge of a

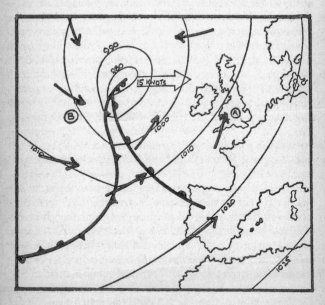

Figure 31

A typical depression

warm front—the Eastern edge of the wedge—is indicated by a half circle similarly placed on the advancing side of the Front.

Isobars may well look like the example in Figure 31 as a depression deepens and the cold front begins to catch up the warm front.

The apex of the wedge is the centre of the depression where the minimum pressure is situated. It will be seen that the isobars as they approach the centre tend to get closer together which results in strong winds flowing in an anticlockwise direction (cyclonic).

How is all this going to be of use to you or I with our proposed weekend dinghy sailing? A splendid starting point could be the weather forecast chart which is given daily on page two of the *Times* newspaper. It covers an area of some fifteen hundred miles West and East of the British Isles, and plots the centres of high pressure, and the depressions. You can see them advancing from the West, these depressions, and while here in England we may be experiencing weather associated with the Maritime Polar air mass—good visibility, fairly steady high barometer and cumuliform clouds giving occasional showers— about six hundred miles from the approaching Front we may well begin to detect cirrus clouds (commonly known as 'mares tails') very high in the sky, perhaps some five miles up. The wind at this time may well be from a South Westerly direction and of moderate strength as you would expect in position (A) on Figure 31.

As the depression approaches from the West so the barometer will begin to fall, and the wedge of warm air which is floating up the inclined face of the cold air it is replacing, becomes thicker. The cirrus clouds will increase and form what is known as cirro-stratus. The high air becomes hazy and it is in this type of cloud formation that haloes around the sun and moon may be observed. It is a sure sign of disturbed weather approaching. The wind backs (moves anticlockwise) and strengthens. The barometer will continue to fall until the actual Front passes across and the faster the barometer falls the stronger may the expected wind be. A fall of one millibar per hour can mean winds of up to gale force.

The cirro-stratus cloud thickens downwards and alto-stratus (often called a 'watery sky') begin to form. This is a level sheet of cloud at medium height usually grey in colour. If this is thick enough rain will begin to fall because the body of warm moisture-soaked air has had to cool by being forced up above the cold wedge, which results in what is called 'precipitation', or rain as you and I would call it. The warm front at ground level may now be some two hundred miles West of us and the whole depression could be moving at a rate of ten or twenty knots Eastward.

As the warm front gets closer nimbo-stratus clouds (generally dark grey) give continuous rain or snow and poor visibility, with the wind tending to strengthen until the actual ground-level of the Front passes. It can get up to gale force, and the lower parts of the nimbo-stratus often become detached and form loose 'scud' which, alas, we often experience during the sailing season in the British Isles.

Ground level of the warm Front will now be with us and the barometer will tend to remain at a steady low pressure. The wind—previously Southerly—will veer (swing clockwise) and blow from a South Westerly or Westerly direction. Rain may ease or stop and the temperature rise. There may also be an increase in humidity and in early summer when the water temperature is quite low a sea fog often forms. We can expect fair, dull, or bright but muggy conditions.

The cold front which is now approaching is nearly always steeper in its inclination than the warm front which has already passed. So the change of weather conditions at this cold front are likely to be more violent than those already felt at the warm front. As the cold front passes polar air is replacing tropical air and the centre of the depression will be moving away to the East or North East. The barometer often starts to rise rapidly as pressure increases and temperature falls. Winds will veer again suddenly, this time to the North West, gusty in strength and treacherous in direction. Since the warm moist air is being forced up the steep incline of the cold front very rapidly, cumulus and cumulo-nimbus clouds are condensed giving local heavy rain. These are the bulbous, flat-bottomed clean-edged clouds that look altogether too solid to stay up there. Thunder and squally winds are likely, but it is all a sign of better weather to come as the cold front moves across to the North East and here again we may well see the high cirrus or 'mares tails' marking the depression's trailing edge, just as it marked its advancing edge.

So our weather again settles down to that associated with a Maritime Polar air stream with winds moderating and blowing from anywhere between North West and South West, until the next bulge develops in the Polar Front to the West of us.

It often happens that at the centre of a depression the advancing cold front has already caught up with the warm front which was ahead of it, in which case the warm lighter air will have been lifted completely off the earth's surface. This is called an occlusion, and it starts at the centre of a depression and moves outward along the line of the warm front rather like the curved blades of a pair of shears closing. On the weather chart this line of occlusion is indicated by alternate triangles and half circles. If the depression has already occluded before reaching us we can expect to experience much the same changes in the weather pattern as it passes, except that there will be no warm sector between the two Fronts. This is already up in the air and will pass over our heads. Once the occlusion becomes extended the depression will start filling up. The barometer will rise, and a fairly stable and relatively high pressure airstream will result.

Of course these depressions do not always pass cleanly across the British Isles to give the weather pattern just described. Sometimes they move North of us, sometimes South, but from intelligent interpretation of the weather chart we ought to be able to make an inspired guess as to whether it's worth getting the boat out of mother-in-law's garage on Friday night or carry on with the decorating!

The exact direction of movement of these depressions is very difficult to forecast and may be strongly influenced by high airstreams and the proximity of anticyclones ('high') and other depressions etc. The illustration in Figure 32 shows in elevation the sort of conditions which may be expected during the passage overhead of a depression, but it is only in the Meteorological offices where full information is available of wind conditions at all altitudes that inspired guesses may reasonably be expected to come true.

The whole weather pattern in these Temperate Latitudes is most complex and greatly influenced locally by the unequal heating of the air over land and sea. As already mentioned, when there is little overall cloud cover the land tends to heat up during the day more quickly than does the sea. The air above it becomes heated causing a local updraught which results in a sea-breeze coming off the water during the day.

At night the land cools more quickly than the sea which tends to cause the reverse—localised high pressure above the land resulting in a breeze toward the sea. Over large land masses these local convectional disturbances can cause brisk winds. In a really well established 'high' or anticyclone the winds which are spiralling outward in a clockwise direction can be up to force 4 or 5 of the Beaufort Scale given in Figure 33, but they do tend to be steady and not as gusty as winds of similar strength in the wake of a cold front.

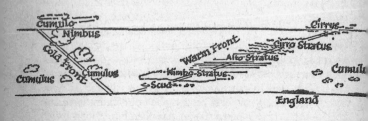

Figure 32

Cross section of a depression
along the line (A) - (B) in Figure 31

ANTICYCLONES

These are more likely to bring conditions conducive to being on the beach—and therefore a beginner's sailing weather—than the depressions.

Unlike a depression which, once it has started has a fairly predictable course of events, an anticyclone is more indeterminate. In essence the anticyclone is an isolated bit of a high pressure belt and may in one aspect be thought of as opposite to a depression in so far as the air is tending to subside—sink slowly. This tends to inhibit convection which is why anticyclonic weather is fairly stable.

Assuming that by observation of a weather chart we see that we are on the edge of a high pressure area, the winds we are experiencing will probably be at least moderate in force, but remaining steady in whatever direction they are blowing.

There may be a marked haze at ground level which is a sign that the anticyclone is well established. Whatever weather is with us at the time will probably continue because an anticyclone is a huge, slow moving mass of air. By looking at a weather chart a person not expert in weather lore will not be able to tell in which direction it is likely to develop.

If the observer is sitting in the centre of an anticyclone the weather pattern will be stable but the winds will be much lighter and variable, and the reason for their variable nature is that local convectional disturbances (i.e. sea-breezes) are able to superimpose themselves on the overall pattern.

In such circumstances the unwary yachtsman, seeing a sea-breeze develop due to the heating of the land may proceed out to sea—possibly on an ebb tide from an estuary—thinking that the sea-breeze will always bring him back. With the cooling of the land at evening however this breeze will die and he may be left with a long row back against the ebb tide in this case!

On a quiet, typical 'anticyclonic' day therefore it often pays an estuary sailor to launch early and go seaward to pick up this developing sea-breeze as soon as possible, for often one can get a decent sailing breeze near an estuary mouth long before it penetrates into the upper reaches of the river. All the same, he must not be too confident and rely on this just in case it does not in fact develop. The onset of these sea-breezes can be quite sudden and by mid-afternoon may easily be moderate to fresh in strength diminishing as the evening comes in.

The long period of settled weather in an anticyclone should not be confused with a ridge of high pressure which is merely a relative area of high pressure sandwiched between two 'Lows' and this travels with the 'Lows'.

An anticyclone which is declining will show a disappearance of the haze at low levels while the wind remains light. This process may take a day or two. But an anticyclone which is moving away will retain the haze but show the fact by an increasing wind strength. If you propose going outside the bounds of an estuary it's wise to be wary of this haze for it can develop almost to the point of fog.

On weather maps or in shipping forecasts on the radio, wind speeds may be given in nautical miles per hour (knots), or reference may be made to what is known as the Beaufort Wind Scale as follows:

Figure 33

Beaufort Wind Scale

Beaufort Force	Wind speed in knots	Wind description, and reaction of a dinghy helmsman
0	Less than one knot	Calm. Not worth sailing.
1	1–3	Light airs. A drifting match.
2	4–6	Light breeze. Just worth sailing.
3	7–10	Gentle breeze. Can now begin to feel the boat.
4	11–16	Moderate breeze. Sailing is stimulating.
5	17–21	A fresh breeze. The inexperienced wisely begin to discover defects in their boats. The experienced become enthusiastic and cause defects in their boats.
6	22–27	A strong breeze. All but madheads go home. Others unstep their masts and secure the boat to the ground.
7	28–33	Near gale. Go home.
8	34–40	Gale. Scrutinise insurance policy.
9	41–47	Strong gale. Not often experienced in England.
10	48–55	Storm. We read about it in the papers for days.
11	56–63	Violent storm.
12	Above 63	Hurricane.

Remember that shipping forecasts give wind details for the open sea and this will be influenced by the type of land in close proximity to your sailing area. It will of course be diverted by headlands and will tend to speed up when blowing into or out of a narrow estuary.

A tidal stream when running in the same direction as the wind will result in a fairly calm water surface. With the change of the tide however, when it begins to run against the wind there will be a marked disturbance of the surface which may lead you to think that the wind has increased when in fact it has done nothing of the sort. But remember that when out there on the water your boat is moving relative to the water and wind, so in fact your own relative wind WILL have increased from the sailing point of view. When you come ashore however you will wonder what all the fun was about!

It's always a good idea (especially if your sailing is going to involve much travelling time) to listen to the B.B.C. forecast for your area and if you plan any specific trip, such as along a coast, the telephone number of your local Met. Office is given at the front of the telephone directory under the heading 'Facilities and Services'.

5

Buying a Boat

Once the newcomer to sailing has mastered the rudiments, possibly after taking a short course at a sailing school, he is faced with the very real problem of how best to acquire a boat and more important still—which boat to acquire.

If one has learned to sail in any particular class of boat it's a fact that, due simply to one's ignorance of other classes, one tends to think that this is the boat which suits one best. Of course this isn't necessarily so and I always advise a beginner to refrain at least for one season from buying a boat and to make and take every opportunity to crew and helm as wide a variety of classes as possible.

This may be done by becoming known at the local sailing club or cultivating the friendship of boat owners and generally making it known that you are prepared to help in the maintenance of the boat, and are keen to crew whoever and wherever possible. If you give service in proportion to the fun you get in sailing other people's boats you will seldom find yourself short of an opportunity to sail. This way you will also quickly discover whether you fall naturally into the bracket of crew or helmsman. In my experience it's often the female sex who choose to crew, while the more aggressive male likes to take control with the tiller in hand!

Some boatyards hire dinghies by the hour, day, or week. While these may be suitable for beginners they are generally slow, stable and heavy craft since the very nature of the business is wide open to misuse of the boats which have to look after the user, rather than the reverse. Sometimes, alas, the condition of boat and equipment leaves much to be desired and it is a wise precaution before taking a hire boat out to check that the obvious items such as halyards, sheets, and standing rigging are in a serviceable condition.

As a beginner I would not advise borrowing a friend's boat unless the friend is there with you and supervising things, because with the best will in the world sheer lack of experience in handling the boat will inevitably result in a straining of the equipment and possible damage to the hull.

I think the best method of gaining this experience is to contact a friend who already owns a boat, or seek out a member of the local sailing club and make an outright offer to share the expenses and labour of maintaining the boat in return for the chance to crew and occasionally helm her.

After one season like this you will have formed an opinion of the pattern your sailing is likely to take. Is it racing, or pottering? Do you prefer the companionship and teamwork of a crew, or are you a 'loner'?

Is your home near the water or will you have to trail the boat? All these things will influence your decision, but perhaps the most important factor governing the choice will be a consideration of the classes sailed at your local Club.

Unless you really are a 'loner' who enjoys sailing for the sheer delight of handling the boat oneself and getting away from the crowd, it will probably be best to choose a class raced at the local Club. If possible get proposed and seconded for entry into the Club for there is much to be said for mixing with owners of boats similar to your own. You'll learn a lot from listening to the devotees of a Class discussing the latest fittings and modifications to the Class rules, and the pros and cons of various sailmakers and boatbuilders. It's all part of the fun of sailing.

For the young and lissom teenager the lightweight sailing surfboard type of dinghy which can be put on a car roof-rack and handled down a beach or hard by one person has a strong appeal. In a fresh breeze these are fast and exciting craft, but one tends to be in the water almost as much as on it, and you may soon find yourself strangely interested in wetsuits if you are going to continue enjoying sailing such a boat in these

Northern climes. The greatest appeal of this type of boat is that it falls into the lowest price bracket with do-it-yourself kits available from £80 odd and the finished boat ready to sail costing in the region of £110 upwards.

Moving up the scale in size the popular two-man dinghies of from eleven to fourteen feet in length are versatile in that they may be trailed behind a car and still handled up a beach by helmsman and crew. These boats weigh generally between 180lbs and 300lbs, and I know many owners whose final choice of boat was governed by the fact that they could without assistance roll the boat on boat rollers up and down the beach and also position the craft on the trailer without the help of any other than their crew. The tremendously popular eleven foot Mirror can also be put on a car roof, and kits are available from £75 or the complete boat for under £120. The fourteen foot G.P.14, a long established and sturdy two-man dinghy costs from £275, while the thirteen foot three inch Enterprise, perhaps the most prolific of all two-man dinghies, is available from about £275 also.

The family man who must cater for perhaps up to five people wishing to sail at the same time will have to resign himself to either leaving the boat on a mooring afloat, or calling for assistance in launching and getting the boat on to a trailer on shore. Such a boat—probably in the region of sixteen feet in length—will generally weigh in excess of 350lbs, and while it is still quite easy to trail them, the sheer weight does discourage handling the boat ashore. The Wayfarer, used as the example of a good family dinghy throughout this book, weighs 370lbs stripped, and costs from about £420.

You will be well advised to get a secondhand boat for your first purchase because you will still be in a state of development regarding prowess on the water, and although you may well have already decided that a particular class best suits your requirements it's my experience that the first season in one's own boat focuses a still wandering inclination as to which will be your final choice. Having bought secondhand you'll stand to lose far less—indeed it is possible to gain on the resale of a boat if you are prepared to increase her value by putting in some hard work in order to enhance her appearance.

When buying a class boat you are well advised to ensure that she has a valid measurement certificate and if not, tell the owner that you may purchase subject to her passing measurement. Most Clubs have an official measurer attached to them who will undertake this for a fee which is laid down in the Class Rules, and of course you can deduct this from the price asked for the boat if you do decide to buy. If the boat does not pass measurement you will not be able to race her at many Club events, and you will also find greater difficulty in re-selling her. Boats built from kits by amateurs, or from basic plans, are particularly suspect and you will be in a strong position when bargaining over price of a secondhand dinghy if the owner does not hold a valid measurement certificate and is not willing to obtain one.

Finally, the question of glassfibre or wood? The obvious advantage of glass is that it virtually precludes the sort of superficial maintenance necessary to the hull and decks of a wooden boat, and for that reason alone this material is gaining tremendous popularity. A modern plywood dinghy of say fourteen to sixteen feet in length will probably cost in the region of £40 per year if properly maintained by a good boat-yard. This can of course be drastically reduced if you're prepared to put in the hours of labour yourself but it does take skill and experience to refit a boat properly—knowing how much to sand off the existing varnish and paint and in what manner, and what type of paint and varnish to apply is half the battle.

Aesthetically one may be prejudiced toward wooden boats—there is a beauty in the graining and joinery work which some of us miss in a glass hull, but it does tend to be a rather expensive prejudice if you just have not the time to do your own refitting.

CARE OF YOUR BOAT

Consider the sails first. As already stated there is more wear and tear on a suit of sails occasioned by leaving them flogging in the wind when a boat is on the beach or at a mooring than will be caused by days of sailing where the cloth is properly filled with wind. I have seen the bottom of batten pockets in a brand new terylene sail split and tear the stitching within thirty minutes of the sail being hoisted for the first time. The flogging puts an unfair strain on the bottom end of the batten pocket due to the stiffness of the batten and this is almost always the first place to show signs of wear and tear, closely followed by the stitching along the leach near the head.

Slackness in tacking will eventually result in similar trouble for you will appreciate that if a tack is executed badly and the sail is allowed to flog for longer than necessary as the boat tacks, the cumulative effect on the sail is identical. Partly for this reason, and partly to ensure that the boat spends the minimum possible time with power switched off, I always harden my mainsheet when tacking.

Often I have heard inexperienced helmsmen remark in a stiff breeze that they 'could not get her through the wind'. This is nonsense: the brisker the wind the easier and quicker should be the tack unless something is seriously wrong with the design. The reason why a well designed boat does not succeed in tacking in a brisk wind is almost certainly because the helmsman has failed to harden his mainsheet as he puts the helm decisively down. By so doing the stern of the boat is kicked to leeward, pivoting the hull round the centreboard and the sail picks up the wind again on the opposite side at the earliest possible moment to start driving again.

Regarding storage of sails, while mould will form on terylene cloth it does not affect the strength. Still, it makes it unsightly so as a principle when storing the sails you ought to ensure the maximum possible circulation of air round the cloth. Never bundle a wet sail into the sailbag and stuff the wet sheets in on top, to leave them for a week until you next need them. They'll not be 'sweet' when you take them from the bag again and I have known the most unhealthy smell develop after sheets had been wetted with salt water and confined in a closed space for a day or so.

It is rare today for cotton sails to be used but if you have a suit they will require considerably more care than terylene. If soaked in salt water it is necessary to rinse them in fresh water and then dry thoroughly on a clothesline—but NOT in a strong wind—before stowing them away. And even when they are thoroughly dry they fare much better bundled loosely or hung from a beam perhaps so that fresh air can flow round the cloth. Sea water allowed to dry off in strong sunshine will leave a deposit of salt on the cloth and when the atmosphere becomes humid the sails will become damp again. Always remove the battens from their pockets after use because they will be under slight tension in the pockets and this is not conducive to a good looking sail if left permanently in. Remember too that the shape of a sail may be ruined by thoughtless mishandling. I have in mind the hard-fisted helmsman who, using a three-fold purchase system of blocks on the mainsheet hardens his sheet until the poor leach is groaning with the strain. Such people seem to think they'll propel the boat along by sheer strength even though the wind be light! It's quite wrong, and indeed in light airs you'll get far more propulsion out of the wind by easing the sheets a trifle so that the sail develops a nice rounded aerofoil shape and it will pay you not to try to sail as close as you would expect in these conditions.

By all means harden your mainsheet in brisk winds but if you do so you will get far better performance by allowing the lower block to slide to the extremity of the sheethorse track. Many boats have control lines fitted to quickly adjust the amount of slide at the lower block. As a general principle the block should be restricted to the centre section of the sheethorse in light airs, and allowed the full traverse in strong winds.

If your boat is a high performance dinghy the mainsail may have a Cunningham hole eye about two feet up the luff to which will be attached a lanyard for hauling down on the eye. This draws the belly or 'draught' of the sail forward towards the luff and while maintaining the aerofoil curve at the luff it flattens the sail which is desirable in brisk winds. The performance is noticeably improved but of course it does only apply in brisk winds. Here again you must remember that you are dealing with a delicate thing and it's not always maximum strength which achieves maximum performance. You must get a feel for your sails just as you must develop a feel for your boat and they will both give you many more years of first class performance than they would otherwise.

Apart from the batten pockets and leach of the mainsail the

next point to show signs of wear will probably be the luffrope, particularly at the head. Each time the sail is hoisted the cloth at the luff is chafed as it slides up the track in the mast. Watch this point and if there are signs of wear at the end of the season send it to a reputable sailmaker for all the necessary repairs. Don't wait until a week before you wish to launch the boat in the Spring because he'll be so busy you'll be lucky to have it back by midsummer!

The jib suffers most at the clew and leach because here again it is these points which flog most, particularly during the tack. The correct handling of the sail can eliminate this flogging and I always instruct my crew to keep the jibsheet taut when executing a tack because, if handled intelligently the jib can greatly assist by being momentarily back-winded as the boat goes through the eye of the wind. The strain should then be taken on the lee sheet just before the weather sheet is let fly and the sail is then working throughout the whole tack except for that one split second when the plane of the sail is parallel to the airstream.

Correct positioning of the jibsheet leads is not only conducive to good performance but also to a longer life for the sail. If you imagine a line extending back from the clew of the sail which would be an extension of the line bisecting the angle at the clew, and then come five or seven degrees down from this imaginary line—that's the correct line for the jibsheet to follow. By so doing it imparts slightly more downward pull on the leach than horizontal pull on the foot, and this is what is required since the leach is much longer. If the sheetlead is too far aft the leach will tend to flutter and you won't have to do much sailing like that before the stitching wears out!

When stowing the jib remember it has a wire rope sewn into the luff and although this is very flexible it is a bad policy to bend it sharply for this may result in a more or less permanent kink in the wire. Start at the head of the sail and roll the wire in a coil until the tack is reached. But if you are stowing it away for a long period it's far better to hang the sail up as already mentioned.

What of the mast? If this is of alloy it will almost certainly be gold-anodised or similarly treated to prevent corrosion. If the spar is wood, it will need a protective coat of varnish each season and you will find that the point of most wear is that area adjacent to the gooseneck. It frequently shows a black bruising of the wood here, sometimes because the jibsheets are attached to the clew of the sail with a metal shackle—a practice I loathe. When the sail is flogging in brisk winds that small shackle becomes a fiendish weapon which can knock out an eye. Also, when tacking the shackle may well clout the mast each time resulting in the aforementioned bruising. I put an overhand knot each side the clew cringle of my jib and eliminate the need for the shackle. This bruise on the mast is often augmented by knocking the wood with the metal plate at the tack of the boom when hoisting the main, and also by the inboard end of the whisker pole if incorrectly handled. It's all conducive to wear and tear at this lower end of the mast and if you are tackling the revarnishing yourself you may be tempted to scrape deep to remove the marks for appearances sake. Be careful—it is weakening the soft wood at a point where a great deal of thrust is imparted by the boom and if you scrape it every season you may well find your mast has a wasp waist at this critical point.

In a wooden mast the track up which the luffrope slides is very delicate and gets badly worn at the lower end until you find the luffrope is entering the track quite a few inches up the mast. This is the beginning of a rapid deterioration in the track, for inevitably you will one day find you have hoisted your main quite a distance with the top of the luffrope in the track and the rest of it out of the track! This prises the track jaws apart, and makes it easier ever after to repeat the fatal process. Have a fillet of hardwood such as oak or mahogany or ash scarfed into the first six inches or so of the track. Once the luffrope is introduced and held in this first section it will not pull out of the track in the softwood above unless the mast is quite beyond further service.

The same comments regarding the wooden mast track apply to the wooden boom track for the footrope. The point most worth noting here is that when bending on the sail to the boom, having inserted the tack pin and correctly tensioned the foot of the sail by means of the clew-outhaul line the latter should be taken at least one turn round beneath the boom and back through the eye so that it is the line which takes the strain and not the delicate track in the boom.

The ideal method of storing a mast and boom is to hang it by one end so that no bending strain is imposed on the spar. But few households have a room available for this purpose some 25 feet in height, and the next best method of storage is a rack with as many suspension points as possible which are completely level and broad on their faces. Even then it's good to turn the spar as often as possible so as to counteract the gravity-bends! One can very easily give a permanent bend to a spar by thoughtless storage over the winter.

As to the boat's hull, if this is of wood or marine ply there will almost certainly be more deterioration taking place when the boat is not sailing during the season than when she is. To leave a boat ashore with the bungs in and no watertight cover is inviting trouble. She will fill with water from the sky, and leaves too if there are any trees about. Within a week you'll have a miniature duckpond complete with weeds. Always remove the bungs and all the inspection hatches of the built-in buoyancy tanks. If the bungs are in the transom—which they usually are —see that the boat is angled up at the bow so that any rainwater entering will wash straight down through and leave the boat sweet.

It's the enclosed spaces that give serious trouble first. Water trapped in a locker for a month or two when a boat is laid up will permanently disfigure the appearance of wood and is conducive to rot, though this is not so likely in marine plywood which is incredibly resistant to any delamination or rotting. The same general principle applies for the hull as for the sails— the more clean dry air which can circulate the better for all concerned.

In summer, when the boat is left on a beach or hard the sun's direct rays can cause a rapid deterioration of decks, and it's always better to have her beneath a roof. Boat covers are a mixed blessing, for with the best will in the world there will be some slight seepage during a heavy rainstorm where the cover laces round the mast, or round the shrouds and along the fore-deck etc. Once inside the water will evaporate when the sun comes out again, but it cannot easily escape again so there is a sort of humid oven of damp air trapped inside and it doesn't help! P.V.C. covers do this even more than canvas types, and it's my opinion that unless the boat is to be left where there is a great deal of dust and grit in the air, she may well be better without a cover provided the water can drain cleanly away.

Children on a beach can be a pest. No: let's be honest, the children are not really to blame because who WOULDN'T play sandcastles and pirates and Admirals at a young and tender age when there's a socking great real boat to do it in! But the parents stand and watch them! Boats on beaches seem strangely to become a part of the local amenities like trees and prom- enade seats. Ye Gods! I was once so furious at finding my immaculate Wayfarer plastered in mud that I went and deliber- ately ate my sandwiches on the bonnet of the offenders parent's car. He was speechless the peculiar man!

It's well worth giving the decks two good coats of marine varnish every season even though you may feel them to be 'good enough for another year'. No matter how good the finish appears to be, at the end of a season there will be wear points where the backs of one's thighs and calves have rubbed the varnish from the inner edges of the side-decks. The edges of the centreboard case and the thwarts and all other parts which get friction will also probably be down to bare wood and water will then quickly penetrate the grain and discolour it. This will call for careful scraping back to bright wood before revarnish- ing, but be warned—you cannot repeat this too often on ply surfaces or you will go right through the surface veneer. It will shriek at you for evermore!

It's commonsense that such equipment as bottom boards from the cockpit, hatch covers, buoyancy bags, oars, paddles etc. should be removed from the boat when she is finally stored for these all tend to trap moisture and delay quick evaporation with consequent discolouration of the wood.

If you are tackling the repainting of the hull be advised that it is in the preparation that the hard work lies. It is all too easy to fall for the temptation and just apply one quick coat of gloss enamel after a quick sanding down of the paintwork. This is bad practice. There will be scores, gouges and hair cracks in the old paintwork and to do a really good job it's necessary first to wash the whole hull down with fresh water and allow it to dry thoroughly again if you intend to sand down with dry sandpaper. The purpose of this sanding down is just to remove any flaking paint and abraid the surface of the old enamel so that the new coat can key. Having sanded down all dust should be removed (a vacuum brush does this well) and the scores and cracks filled with a filler which any good chandler will supply. Allow this to dry and then sand off the local surfaces which have been filled until you have it all perfectly level with no filler standing proud of the surface.

Apply undercoat to all the filled surfaces and when this is dry it's best to give the whole hull one coat of undercoat. A clean dry atmosphere free of dust is essential. Spring is a good time because there are few flies and the atmosphere is free of dust but the sun is warm enough to allow quick drying. Should the undercoat have any evident roughness due to grit or other impurities, very lightly sand these off with a fine grade sandpaper and remove all loose dust again. Then apply the final coat of enamel, using the same type of paint as originally applied. This may be two-can polyurethane, one-can polyurethane, or normal marine enamel but you must know which because the type of filler and undercoat varies.

If the painting is to be done in the open choose the day and time of commencing with care. In Spring you will be best to start the final painting at about eleven a.m. and complete the job by two-thirty at the latest otherwise the coat may not have hardened sufficiently before evening damp sets in. Choose a day when there is a little chance of rain, and this does not necessarily mean brilliant sunshine for too much of this around lunchtime can blister the paint!

With regard to varnish work on deck and the interior skin of the boat you will not of course use a filler unless there is a serious gouge in the woodwork, and then the filler should be coloured so as to match the colour of the wood. Rub briskly down so as to remove any flaking varnish, and apply a coat of the same type of varnish as originally used to all bare places. When this is completely dry, very lightly sand down these newly varnished places and apply an overall coat to the complete surface. For a really good job, when this is thoroughly dry very lightly sand down the whole surface with fine grade sandpaper and after removing every trace of dust flow on a final coat of varnish to give deep protection. But you must not expect varnish ever to give quite the protection afforded by enamel since by its very nature it is transparent to sunlight and therefore the surface beneath is always subject to discolouration by penetration of the sun's rays. It fades to a lighter colour as the years go by.

Use a good quality marine varnish and do not try to be penny wise and pound foolish in your choice of paints. The final result obtained by the home refitter depends on experience and knack just as much as enthusiasm and good intention linked with hard work. Some people can paint and some just cannot: you should know which bracket you fall into. If it's the latter take my advice and let the job be done by a professional. It will cost you more than you think you can afford, but if you really care for your boat it will be worth it.

As to glassfibre, there is little you can do to maintain it, and if we are to believe the manufacturers little you need to do. But I have examined the outside skins of many glassfibre boats of two or three years age and observed that they too are prone to scoring of the surface caused by rubbing on pebbles and general abrasion through normal use. This need not cause alarm, but it is not conducive to good looks. It is, of course, quite possible to coat the hull exterior with polyurethane paint after necessary preparation to ensure good keying, but this brings one back to annual maintenance and after all the point of buying a glass boat was to avoid this.

Serious structural damage such as a hole (unlikely in a glass hull due to its incredible toughness) can be repaired either professionally or with a 'do-it-yourself' kit. But if the hull colour is pigmented you will probably find difficulty in exactly matching the slightly faded colour of the original shell. Merely getting the same pigmentation as the original boat does not always suffice because sunlight plays funny tricks with colours and generally you'll find that the old skin is a shade or so lighter than the new 'infill'. I have seen nearly perfect repairs to fibreglass hulls, but must add that these have always been effected by a professional boatbuilder.

Violent changes of temperature such as hot summer midday sun and cold nights will be conducive to expansion and contraction breakdown of the gelcoat surface. This may not be immediately evident to the naked eye but it results in myriads of microscopic hair cracks and this is all a part of the slow but inexorable process of breakdown of the glassy surface. So do not think that glassfibre is everlasting: it's not, but it will probably last longer in a deplorable condition than wood! There will have to eventually be an International Agreement way on in the future to jettison every fibreglass disused boat-hull in some deep ocean chasm, otherwise we shall probably be climbing over them immediately we open the front door.

But joking aside, for the man who has no time to spare for giving loving care to a thing of beauty and craftsmanship, there's no doubt that the glass hull and deck is a boon. You can leave it in the back garden for the frogs to spawn in, hose it down in the Spring—and you're sailing! Mind you: you must not let the rainwater freeze in it otherwise this really can disrupt things.

TRAILING DINGHIES

Your decision as to which dinghy you buy will have been influenced by where you are able to sail her. If she is suitable to keep on a mooring—very stable, unlikely to capsize by windage on the mast alone—or perhaps if she can be left safely on a hard or beach, then you may not need a trailer for you can probably borrow or hire one for the two occasions in the year when the boat has to be brought back home. But if you are going to explore many different lakes and estuaries then you will need a road trailer.

First make sure your car is capable of towing the overall weight of boat and trailer. If in doubt check with your garage or some other reliable source.

Any trailer stockist will advise you on the correct trailer for your boat. The main thing is that the hull must be well balanced on the trailer and supported in the correct places. So the length of the trailer is important and the weight of the boat must be distributed evenly either side the axle with a slight tendency to drop down at the nose. Many trailers have adjustable axle positions and adjustable side chocks to support the hull at the bilge keels on either side.

Having decided on the trailer check the size of the ball coupling thereon and make sure you fit the same size ball hitch to your car. These used to be two inches in diameter, but the Continental size of 50 millimetres is now superseding them and it's best to have the latter because it will be standard size shortly. The garage will fit the towbar and ball hitch for you.

In Chapter 3 I explained the method of loading the boat on to a launching trolley. The same applies to a road trailer. Some trailers are fitted with a keel rear roller on which the boat

Are you sure you put
the spare battens in
Darling?

can roll forward more easily, and for bigger dinghies a winch can be fitted to the fore end of the trailer which greatly assists loading and unloading—particularly when on a steep slipway.

When the boat is correctly sited on the trailer with her weight taken mainly on the bow and stern rollers and a moderate amount also bedded on the side chocks, she must be securely lashed in position. If there is no forward 'bumper' on the trailer (generally a rubber cushion fixed to the vertical mast support at the front) the boat must be prevented from sliding forward against the car if the latter stops suddenly. Similarly she must be lashed so as to prevent sliding off the back when the car quickly accelerates. Secure lashings are particularly needed when the roller type chocks are fitted as these do facilitate movement. The mast support (generally an extra to the trailer price) is fitted at the forward end so as to keep the top of the mast above the roof of the car. The rear end of the spar should be cushioned and securely lashed to the transom.

Having verified the towing capacity of the car, loaded the boat correctly with due regard to weight distribution and adjusted the mast on the support, some owners make the mistake of assuming they have an extra luggage carrier at the rear. Into the boat go the suitcases and golf clubs that overflow from the boot, and sometimes the outboard motor Heaven forbid! Well ... there's nothing wrong with putting the odd piece of light gear into the boat, but do remember the care you took to distribute her weight correctly and check that the 'all up' weight has not exceeded the maximum recommended for the trailer. Stow the extra bits and pieces somewhere near the axle, and secure it to prevent sliding during transport.

A spare wheel and jack is useful when on a really long distance tow, and can make the difference between getting to a race meeting in time, or just missing the event for which you've been practising for months! If you have never trailed before I would suggest a bit of practice before going on the busy roads: especially in reversing. Make sure, too, that you comply with the Law, a summary of which is given below:

THE LAW ON TRAILING DINGHIES

This is given in full in the H.M.S.O. publication 'The Motor Vehicles (Construction and Use) Regulations 1969', and items of these Regultaions which normally apply to the driver of a family saloon car towing a dinghy are as follows.

A private car may not tow more than one trailer.
Length of the trailer must not exceed 22 feet 11½ inches (7 metres) excluding the draw-bar.
Width of the trailer must not exceed 7 feet 6 inches.
Tyres must be inflatable and each wheel must be equipped with suitable and sufficient springs.
Brakes are not required on trailers weighing less than two hundredweight unladen.
Trailer wheels must be fitted with wings to catch water and mud thrown up by their rotation.
Maximum speed when trailing is 40 miles per hour.

If the overhang of the boat exceeds 3 feet 6 inches the person in charge of the towing vehicle must make the projection clearly visible to other road users. A flapping rag is usual in the case of a mast end. Should the overhang exceed more than ten feet then specifically approved signs have to be affixed to the rear, and the police informed before a journey is made.

There must be rear lights on the trailer, plus 'reflex' reflectors and illumination for the number plate. All must be positioned within 30 inches from the back of the trailer load. Rear lamps must not be more than 16 inches from the side of the vehicle and separated by at least 21 inches. Rear lamps and reflectors should not be nearer the road surface that 15 inches nor higher than 42 inches.

Direction indicators need not be fitted when the car has semaphore arm type indicators. If the car is fitted with flashing lights and was registered before the 1st September 1965 then

(1) if the trailor (unladen) weighs less than 2 hundredweight or was constructed before the 1st January 1955, indicators need not be fitted.

(2) Otherwise indicators are necessary but the rear indicators on the drawing car may be dispensed with.

In the case of a car registered after 1st September 1965 the trailer must be fitted with amber coloured indicators and the car must also have them. The only exception is where the trailer is a broken down vehicle, or where the rearmost point of the trailer is less than 12 feet from the rearmost part of the drawing vehicle.

Remember that proper insurance should not be overlooked, and this is a matter best discussed with a broker or the companies insuring both boat and car.

The normal car insurance policy applies (or can be extended to apply) to trailers. Boat and trailer is usually considered to be a trailer for this purpose and Road Traffic Act cover would apply whilst it is being towed by the car.

When detached from the car however no third party cover may be in force as normally the marine third party cover applying to the boat does not apply until the craft is afloat. Similarly, when the trailer is left on its own at the quay side or slipway, no third party cover is applying unless the motor car policy has been specifically extended to include this cover.

The sort of thing I have in mind is when an owner has towed his dinghy to a seaside resort, and having contacted the local Harbourmaster for permission to launch may well find that the car park is a small distance from the slipway. Often the car and boat are driven to the car park when the trailer is unhitched and wheeled by hand along a promenade or public highway (usually packed by holidaymakers) to the slipway for launching. Once the trailer is unhitched from the car no Third Party cover may apply until the boat is actually afloat. This is a critical stage of the manoeuvre when difficulties could arise. Small children for instance, cannot be easily seen behind the boat on its trailer, and injury might result.

It is wise to approach the marine insurers and ask them to extend their policy to include 'manhandling risks'. They are usually pleased to do this for a very small increase in the premium.

Once the boat is afloat of course the marine policy would apply to it, but the trailer—probably left at the top of the slipway and liable to run away on its own—could still cause injury involving the owner in a claim. For this reason it's well worth extending the car policy to apply to the trailer for Third Party risks while it is detached.

6

Coastal Cruising

Only the hardiest and most adventurous of dinghy sailors attempts to navigate his boat in the true sense of the word out in the open sea. Epic voyages have been made in dinghies but these are by experienced sailors who well know the risks they take, cater for them as far as is humanly possible, and then if the voyage ends successfully look upon it as a real achievement to their credit, which it is.

But navigation out of sight of land with sextant, chronometer and nautical tables is for the yachtsman not the dinghywallah, and indeed even coastal pilotage where one checks one's position by compass bearings of objects ashore, and laying off courses to sail, is really beyond the scope of a dinghy helmsman and crew. A small boat heeled and soaked with spray is no place to start laying off courses and plotting 'fixes'.

Nevertheless, when you have fully mastered your boat and always providing your dinghy is suitable for venturing outside the harbour, you may feel competent to make short coastal passages. Having taken all the seamanlike precautions such as checking on the immediate weather forecast, the state of the swell out there in the open sea, and the state of the tide, there's no reason why this should not take place.

But first you really should know how to read a chart intelligently, know how to measure off distances thereon, and be thoroughly familiar with the symbols used to indicate rocks, wrecks, depths and sandbanks which may dry out at low water.

So while it is not my intention to give a course in navigation here, the following pages may come in useful, and anyway it's a fascinating subject. I'm a great believer in understanding why things are as they are—it helps so much in the learning and I've never been able to learn anything by just accepting it as a fact. So let's begin at the beginning.

THE CHART

This is a map of the coastline and the sea. It contains information about objects on shore only if they are useful to a sailor at sea so you will understand why a very short distance inland all the land mass is blank. Soundings of the depth are plotted all over the sea, and these are printed in figures which represent fathoms, a fathom being six feet. Within a few years the term 'fathom' is to be superseded by the metric metre, but at the moment we are sticking to fathoms.

All the depths are given below what is called 'Chart Datum' because you will realise that the depth varies with the state of the tide, and you should be familiar with the meaning of Chart Datum after reading chapter three.

A chart does however suffer from the same unavoidable drawback as a land map—if it covers a large area of the earth's surface it must be subject to distortion. You will realise that to represent any spherical surface such as the face of our earth on to a flat plane some distortion must occur. No matter how hard you try you just can't eliminate this distortion and we must understand this and how it is catered for.

To make the resultant distortion manageable an ingenious system was devised, known as the Mercator Projection. It's very clever.

Imagine the earth to be a glass globe with all the outline of the land masses inked in on the surface. In order to plot a position anywhere on this globe we will have to have some form of grid system using a base line and a vertical, duly graduated like a graph. In the case of our earth the most convenient base line to work from is the equator which is the line running right round the earth equidistant from North and South Poles and dividing the earth into two equal hemispheres.

The vertical line is not so easy to choose: indeed any vertical line would do so long as all navigators know where it is. In point of fact at the time when all this was being worked out

England was a very important maritime nation and it was agreed internationally that the vertical line which passed from Pole to Pole through Greenwich in London and cutting the equator at right angles should be the other reference point. It is called the Prime Meridian.

Imagine the equator and the Prime Meridian to be inked in also on our glass globe. Now one can draw in any number of other Meridians East and West of the Prime Meridian, all passing through the poles and cutting the equator at right angles, and provided we agree upon a form of graduation we can start plotting our position East or West of Greenwich. The best graduation is degrees and minutes of arc. There are 360 degrees in a circle, so if we put in a Meridian at every degree of arc there will be three hundred and sixty Meridians inscribed on the globe, and the Prime Meridian through Greenwich will be referred to as Zero Meridian. This East–West measurement we call Longitude, so instead of saying 'I'm on Meridian 125 deg. West of Greenwich; we simply say 'my Longitude is 125 deg. West' The symbol ° is used to denote 'degrees'.

In practice the degree is subdivided into sixty equal parts and these are called 'minutes'. Nothing whatever to do with time, just one sixtieth of a degree of arc. The symbol for 'minutes' is the sign ′.

In order to establish our distance up and down the Meridians we must of course have similar graduations using the base line at the equator. But since the equator is exactly halfway between the poles we call the equator Zero degrees and graduate up to 90° at North Pole and down to 90° at the South Pole. This graduation up and down the surface of the earth is called Latitude, and if we mark in every line of latitude per degree, we shall see that they are all parallel to each other and all cut every Meridian at right-angles. So there are 180 parallels of Latitude, graduated from 0° at the Equator to 90° at each pole, and 360 Meridians of Longitude graduated from 0° at Greenwich to 180° East and 180° West, and this Meridian (180° East of Greenwich and 180° West of Greenwich) will form the same Meridian diametrically opposite Greenwich Meridian on the opposite side of the earth.

Now, if I say my position is 5° 6′ North and 4° 10′ West it

159

will be possible to plot this point exactly on the surface of the globe, because I know my Latitude and Longitude. Incidentally, when giving a position such as this the Latitude always comes first, followed by the Longitude.

Now look at the imaginary globe again. The outlines of the land masses are inked in, and all the Parallels of Latitude and Meridians of Longitude, and it will be seen that the latter all converge at each pole, and are farthest away from each other at the equator.

But you can't navigate on that globe: it's far too small. This is where the Mercator Projection comes in! The problem is somehow to project that spherical graduated surface on to a flat sheet of paper so that we can still use those divisions of arc without having to make complicated allowances and calculations because of the resultant distortion.

Put a small bright electric light bulb exactly at the centre of the globe. Now imagine a plain sheet of stiff tracing paper to be wrapped round the globe just touching the equator so that it forms a cylinder up whose centre the axis line of the earth lies. Switch on the light. All the black outlines of the land masses and the Parallels of Latitude and Meridians of Longitude will throw a black shadow on to the cylinder. You will see them showing through from the outside.

Think where they will lie, those shadows. The equator line will actually be in contact with the equator on the glass globe, so it completely coincides. The Parallel of Latitude lying say 10° North or South of the Equator will not however be in contact, because the surface of the earth has curved in toward the Pole by then. The shadow will therefore lie a little farther up the paper than it does on the globe. The Latitude line for 20° North will lie, not exactly double the distance from the equator to 10° North, but quite a bit higher up the paper. And so it goes on, each parallel of Latitude getting progressively farther away from its next lower one until of course, 90° North—the actual Pole—will never be projected on to the paper since it lies exactly on the centre line.

What of the Meridians? These will, of course, all cut the equator at right angles but instead of converging to a point at the poles as they do on the globe, the shadows on the paper

160

will simply remain parallel to each other up and down the paper. You can see how this must be by visualising the projection of the shadows by the light.

Ink in all the shadows on the paper and unroll the cylinder from round the globe. We have a Mercator Projection chart of the whole world in front of us on which the graduations on top and bottom edge represents angular distances in degrees and minutes of Longitude AT THE EQUATOR. The graduations up either side of the paper however represent angular distance in degrees and minutes of arc WHEREVER THEY LIE UP THE PAPER, because these are automatically catering for the distortion which has taken place in the projection.

Only one thing remains for us to be able to use this chart of the world. We must find a link between the graduations of arc and actual linear distance on the sea or land. When I tell you that one minute of arc, subtended from the earth's centre, cuts off exactly one nautical mile on the earth's surface you will immediately understand how the whole grid system we have devised becomes of use to us when navigating. One minute of arc is one nautical mile and therefore one degree of arc is sixty nautical miles. In practice a nautical mile is taken as being 2,000 yards, and one cable is one tenth of a nautical mile, or 200 yards.

The circumference of the earth is 360° round at the Equator and therefore we now know that the distance round the earth is 60 × 360 nautical miles, or 21,600 nautical miles. When speaking of distances at sea therefore one always uses the nautical mile and never the land mile which is a quite arbitrary measure of distance some 240 yards shorter!

Looking then at a Mercator chart we will understand that any points we care to plot on the chart using the arguments of Latitude and Longitude will be in their correct relationship to any adjacent land mass just as if we had plotted them on the actual globe, since the distortion which has taken place has affected the land contours as well as the grid lines.

What is most important: you should now understand why, if we wish to find the distance in nautical miles between any two places on the chart, we have to measure this using the scale at either side of the chart and NEVER along the top or

161

bottom. It is also best to use the section of the scale at the same Latitude as the area in which we're navigating otherwise the scale will be slightly wrong for Latitudes much further North or South.

In practice the distortion of this Mercator projection becomes too great above 60° of Latitude and in these Polar regions a different form of projection is used called the Gnomonic Projection. The same system of extending the shadows is used, but instead they are projected on to a flat sheet of paper placed tangentially at the Poles. You will see that in this case the parallels of Latitude come out as concentric circles and the Meridians of Longitude form straight lines radiating out from the Poles rather like the spokes of a peculiar bicycle wheel. If ever you find yourself in need of a chart of Gnomonic projection during your holiday coastal trip in a dinghy, I hope you'll make a mental note to draft a Bankers Order to the Royal National Lifeboat Institution!

Now look at the imaginary Mercator projection chart in Figure 34. It covers an area on the West coast of England between Latitudes 50° 33' and 50° 36' North, and Longitude 04° 58' and 05° 01' West. You will notice immediately that the graduations of minutes of arc at bottom and top are very much closer together than are the graduations up either side of the chart. You now know why.

USE OF TRANSITS

I propose that we wish to go on a trip down the coast some 3½ miles starting from our base in Basket Bay and landing for lunch on Church beach just East of Longnose Point. The object of this imaginary coastal cruise in a dinghy is to show how one may navigate, having looked at the chart before leaving and then taken it with one for quick reference, simply by the intelligent use of transits.

Two objects are said to be in transit when they are both to one side of you and in line with each other. Many people imagine that one can position oneself BETWEEN two objects and then state that one is exactly on the line joining them. It is very inaccurate: practically impossible!

Provided the two objects selected are marked on the chart

this use of transits is more accurate for establishing one's position on the chart than any compass bearing will ever be. It is for this reason that the Port Authorities sometimes erect Leading Marks, which are simply transit posts, duly plotted on the chart. If a vessel coming in from sea keeps the two leading marks exactly in line she knows that she will not foul any offlying dangers such as shoals, rocks or wrecks.

Admiralty Chart number 5011 gives all the symbols and abbreviations used on charts issued by the Hydrographic Dept. of the Admiralty, and from this we will see that a small arrow without any flights on the shaft gives the direction of the ebb tidal stream. On our imaginary chart this is in a Southerly direction down the coast. It will therefore be prudent to start our trip about three hours after High Water which will be about half ebb. The tide will then help us down the coast, speeding our passage. What's more, allowing time for the landing on Church beach we shall be able to start back shortly after Low Water and carry the flood tide back again to Basket Bay.

Before starting such a voyage of course you have listened to the weather forecast and checked with the local Meteorological station for the latest report on conditions likely to develop within the next twelve hours. The telephone number of the local Met. Office is listed under 'Facilities and Services' in the front of the telephone directory and my experience is that they are always keen to help.

Tell somebody responsible ashore exactly what your intentions are, and unless there is good cause to alter your plan— stick to it. Check on all the boat's equipment: buoyancy in good condition, large plastic bucket secured aboard, oars and crutches (rowlocks) or paddles, small compass, serviceable anchor and an adequate length of anchor warp. Daylight distress signal in waterproof container, and of course personal buoyancy will be worn, together with plenty of warm clothing if you take my advice. So, being in all respects ready to proceed let's look at the proposed course.

You will see there are two leading marks at Basket Bay entrance and provided we keep Southward of that transit line we shall clear Bilgehole Rocks just West of the entrance. It will be advantageous to proceed well to sea in order to pick up the

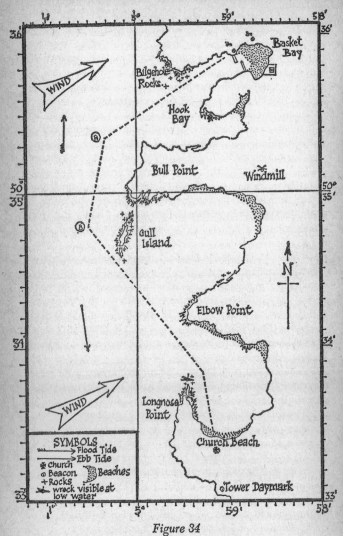

Figure 34

Imaginary chart to illustrate
the use of transits

164

full strength of the ebb tide which might well be sweeping round the curve of Hook Bay and would therefore tend to retard our progress if we sailed too close inshore. Often by keeping close to the shore one can be caught in a tidal stream running directly contrary to the main stream offshore.

So let's take care to sail roughly down the transit line, and since the wind is South Westerly we shall have to ensure when on Port tack not to pass to the North of the leading marks. It's going to be a dead beat to windward on that first leg out of Basket Bay, and the problem is to know when we have reached any preselected point on that line. Visibility is good—we would not be contemplating the cruise if it were not—and by looking at the chart we should realise there is one position on the leading mark transit which can be fixed visually: when Elbow Point first shows clear of Bull Point.

As soon as we see Elbow Point come into view clear of Bull Point we know with absolute certainty that we are in position (A) on the chart and can alter course so as to leave Bull Point well to port. This next leg will bring us close hauled on Starboard tack. The next hazard presenting itself is Gull Island with the submerged rocks Northward toward Bull Point. Obviously if we keep well to seaward of the island there can be no chance of fouling the rocks, but just as a check if we make it our business to notice when the windmill East of Bull Point is in transit with the Southern face of the Point, checking at the same time that the Southern end of Gull island is in transit with Elbow Point to the South, we will have again established our exact position with complete accuracy. At the moment when the two transits coincide we are in position (B).

After that we shall simply sail on a beam reach Starboard tack keeping South of Gull island until well past Elbow Point, when we shall pick up the transit line from the Daymark (a tall tower) on Longnose Point through the Church Tower South of Church beach. This will take us clear of the spit of rocks North of Longnose, and notice there is a wreck which may be a danger at the Northern end of those rocks, all of which may not be showing when we arrive some two hours before Low Water.

The trickiest part may well be the actual landing on the beach. The prevailing wind in the area is West or South West and this tends to knock up a sizeable swell which rolls in from the Atlantic and can break with tremendous force on shallow offshore shoals, and on exposed beaches. Here I want to explain the difference between swell and sea, because we are vitally concerned with the surface conditions on a trip like this. Swell is the name given to that long continuous succession of undulations or rollers one experiences out in deep water. Swell will not break until it meets an obstruction such as rocks or a sloping beach. Its these which make you seasick in a big ship, as they may measure hundreds of yards from crest to crest. They constitute no danger whatever to a small boat in deep water since she simply rises gently and falls again as the swell moves beneath her. Such a swell will have originated at some storm centre far out at sea, tending to emanate in concentric circles from that point. As we approach the beach however we shall be vitally concerned with this swell for it will rise higher and higher as the sea gets shallower near the shore, and finally if the water gets shallow enough it will finally fall over on itself and break with great force. It's no place to be in a dinghy when that's happening, and this is why 'bars'—shallow sandbanks—across the mouths of estuaries are so dangerous at certain states of tide. While the height of tide is sufficient to allow the swell to roll over the bar all is well, but on a falling tide a point is reached where a big swell just cannot manage it and it then breaks with furious power: often just when you least expect it. Keep clear of 'bars' in a dinghy until you really know the area well.

'Sea', on the other hand, is the surface disturbance caused by the friction of the wind and is usually a short, wet choppiness superimposed on top of the swell. The 'sea' varies almost minute by minute with the wind force and a completely calm sea can become very wetting when a brisk wind suddenly springs up. If the sea becomes big a dinghy could founder by being filled with the breaking waves but this is unlikely to happen in winds of under force five to six and you would not choose to go along a coast with that type of forecast looming. Wind against the tidal stream knocks up a bigger sea.

You will detect that we have chosen Church beach as our proposed landing place because it's well protected from the wind by the Northern tip of Longnose Point, and it's also a fair bet that the swell will be rolling in from a South Westerly direction too, having to fan right round to get on to Church beach. In point of fact the beaches at the windmill and South of Elbow Point will probably be experiencing big breakers, but with any luck Church beach should be more hospitable. We may find that while the water level rises up and recedes again

Nothing for it but to press on _and Land!

down the beach, it does not actually break there. But don't be too confident that this will be the case, and on our approach in to the beach we shall keep a wary eye on the situation there. If there is a swell and it's breaking we must discard any idea of landing. Remember that when one is looking ashore from sea-ward one is looking along the backs of the breakers and this can be very misleading for sometimes there appears to be little to worry about. But when you get into them—when it's too late to do anything except press on and land—it can be a different matter. Another point: all the swells which roll in are not the same height. Every seventh or tenth roller tends to be much bigger and it's just one's luck that this will be the one to catch you with your pants down.

On this trip the wind has been, and will be, blowing across the run of the tide both on the flood and on the ebb, so no marked difference in the sea conditions may be expected, but this is something you should bear in mind when planning the day, for if on the trip back the tide should be running against the wind you will have a much sloppier ride and may need to do some bailing!

So coming out of Basket Bay we shall have a head wind and therefore a head-on sea so it will be a wet beat to windward and since we shall still be close hauled from point (A) to (B) we must expect a soaking. From point (B) onward we shall be on a beam reach with the sea on the beam of the boat and we shall be going faster off the wind. It will be invigorating sailing and unless the wind shifts we shall have a good run back. Under the lee of Longnose Point we shall almost certainly lose our wind—taken by the headland—and since there are rocks in the vicinity it will be a seamanlike precaution to have oars or paddles 'at the ready' in case of need. Under the Point the wind will go quite mad, now blowing from one direction and now from another as it swirls and eddies over and round the cliff but by intelligent use of the sails we should be able to sail right on to the beach if we decide to land.

Assuming by long observation we find no swell breaking there we must do this with some skill, for even though there may be no breakers the water will undoubtedly be surging up the inclined beach and falling back again which can make it tricky. The safest method is to drop sails in the lee of the headland and paddle in, but whether we decide to paddle the boat or sail her in we must try to time it so that the boat surges up the beach on the top of a rise. Immediately she touches the beach one member of the crew must jump out and firmly hold on to the bow otherwise the undertow when the water recedes will drag the boat back again into deep water. The other member of the crew should immediately unship the rudder. Once this is done you swing the boat head-to-sea so that the next successive rises will not slop in over the transom and fill the boat. The boat must then be dragged well up the beach clear of all possibility of refloating. Remember that the tide is falling so each successive rise will tend to advance up the beach less distance but you can't rely on that: remember the seventh swell!

Had we beached on a rising tide of course it would have been essential to drag the boat a long way up the beach and put out an anchor just in case. It would have been well worth while to bring along a couple of the boat-rollers to make this easier. Alternatively of course we could have discharged all the picnic gear and anchored the boat well offshore where she would ride safely. That would mean a swim back, and a careful eye would have to be kept on the weather!

Exactly what we do all depends on a seamanlike assessment of the conditions, and I do emphasize once again that safety or disaster at sea nearly always depends on foresight and common sense—or the lack of it. Never take unnecessary risks. This imaginary coastal trip has not been detailed as a recommendation that you undertake such a venture, but simply to acquaint you with the sort of problem you are likely to meet.

Until you know the coast well, or have the benefit of a local seaman's experience with you in the boat, you will be ill advised to attempt it. I would only add that the majority of small dinghies are not suitable for such a passage no matter what the competence of the crew. The Wayfarer is a superb dinghy for this kind of adventure due to her size and seaworthiness.

THE COMPASS

You will have noticed in the above example that no mention, nor use, was made of the compass though we had one in the boat.

This is because I wanted to bring to your attention how, by intelligent use of charted objects ashore you can fix your position with complete accuracy. You will have to have your chart with you in the boat, but frankly all you will be able to do it to give it quick glances to confirm your position on a predetermined course which has all been worked out before-hand on shore.

On such a passage the compass would not be needed, but it would be unseamanlike not to have one in the boat in case of the unexpected arrival of poor visibility—rain or fog. It's up to you to decide, immediately you foresee a chance of this, whether to carry on to the selected destination or make for some intermediate landing point which is safe, or return to your point of departure. The important thing is to make this decision while you can still see your landing place. You must head the boat for that point and note your compass course immediately. You may then lose sight of land completely but you may expect to pick it up again as you get closer. But if there is chance of fog developing you should have abandoned the trip anyway.

There are some excellent small compasses on the market which may be fixed neatly to a dinghy thwart or on the transom or after buoyancy tank face just below the tiller. I favour the small grid-bearing compass it's so much easier to read and detect an error of course while sitting the dinghy out, rather than watching a 'lubbers line' against the card graduation.

7

The Years Ahead

THE DINGHY WITH A LID ON

It is often thought that the jump from sailing a dinghy to sailing a small yacht is a step forward in prowess. With regard to the handling of the boat this is just not the case. It takes far quicker responses and a keener appreciation of the wind and general feel of the boat to sail a dinghy—always liable to capsize—than to sail a yacht. I'm quite sure that the finest training for offshore sailing and ocean voyaging in the true sense of the word is the handling of a small and responsive dinghy.

When you first take the helm of a larger craft you'll almost certainly feel that she is less responsive and in one sense this is true, but really it is that she is responding in a different way. A yacht is not liable to capsize and remain capsized (unless she is a catamaran or trimaran). In extreme circumstances the conventional yacht may be laid over on her beam ends, that is to say with the mast lying along the surface of the water, but she will still (unlike a dinghy) tend to right herself due to the ballast weight in the keel or keels. In a dinghy of course this ballast is just the crew's weight and there does come a point when the dinghy is heeled over that the ballast in form of helmsman and crew can at best do no more than try not to actually assist the capsizing of the boat. It is only after the capsize has taken place that the crew can begin to execute a righting effect by pressure on the centreboard. It isn't so in a yacht. From the first moment when the yacht begins to heel the ballast of the keels starts to attempt to right her, and the maximum righting tendency is reached when the boat is laid horizontally.

It is extremely rare for a conventional yacht to turn 'turtle' —completely upside down—and if she does, provided sufficient buoyancy in the form of air is trapped inside the hull she will soon right herself. If she fills with water in the process of course she will founder, but a seaman engaged in offshore cruising and finding himself where such an event is a possibility will ensure that the hatches are closed and any openings giving access to belowdeck are sealed as far as possible.

In my opinion dinghy sailing is in some ways a rather selfish sport but it may be in this fact that its appeal lies. Helmsman and crew, when they leave the beach or cast off from the mooring are involved in a personal battle, the essence of which is the individual pitting of wits between element and man. There are no passengers to be considered. All aboard are vitally involved in the performance of the boat, or should be.

Once the decision is made to cater for perhaps a family, and one looks for the dinghy with a lid on which can accommodate three or four, your approach to sailing has already changed. Fundamentally you now seek to involve yourself in a way of life which can offer more prolonged escape in the form of a weekend, week, or fortnights holiday in an environ completely different from your normal workaday world. Your horizons widen: instead of the beat to the weather mark you will consider the passage to the next port.

Your responsibilities change. Instead of a thought only of yourself and one crew and at worst the unlikely risk of a five or ten minute dunking, you begin to think in terms of safety of family and passengers, of navigation and seamanship in the true sense of the word. Any man who has mastered the responses of a high performance dinghy and therefore assumes that he's in any way qualified to proceed on a coastal or deep water voyage is frankly an idiot. While there is obviously a link, the two activities largely call for a different kind of skill. Competent navigation and the ability to deal with real violence from the elements in the form of rough seas bears little relation to keeping a dinghy upright in sheltered waters. Anyone thinking of committing himself and those in his charge to the challenge, excitement and achievement of an offshore passage should attend a suitable course of instruction at a sailing school catering for this type of training.

The address of such schools which are approved by the Royal Yachting Association, may be obtained from the Secretary of the R.Y.A. at 5, Buckingham Gate, Westminster S.W.1, or from the Federation of Sailing and Powerboat Schools, at 59 Bath Road, Emsworth, Hants. Such a course will form a good foundation on which to build knowledge and competence which only comes with actual experience. We are, thank Heaven, a seafaring nation, and in my experience it's true to say that in the veriest tyro there is an almost instinctive ability to comprehend and come to terms with the sea in all her moods.

Faced with the problem of which cruising boat to acquire, one very soon realises that the choice is much influenced by a need to compromise. Only those of us with a very deep pocket will be able to afford an offshore cruiser/racer which will remotely tally in performance with a dinghy yet accommodate four or more people in comfort.

You must think about the availability of moorings where you intend to keep the boat. Consider refitting costs, trailability on shore, and the type of harbour from which you will operate coupled with the absolute minimum sleeping accommodation on board.

All this must be linked to your basic intention with regard to the type of cruising you envisage. If you wish to undertake serious deep-sea voyages then you will have to be prepared to sacrifice certain conveniences when in port. For instance a boat able to tackle extended cruising is unlikely to be small and light enough to cart overland. For high performance deep-sea work one really needs a craft with a deep central keel and this means when refit time comes along you will probably have to engage the professional services of a local boatyard to haul her out of the water on a specially constructed cradle. In addition she will have to remain afloat on a deepwater mooring with the attendant need for a small dinghy to board her. Do you then take the dinghy aboard or leave it on the mooring? It's governed by size. The dinghy has to be big enough to safely transport crew and provisions out to the boat in a chop, but small enough to stow aboard without interfering with deckspace too much and the sailing of the yacht.

The part time sailor whose requirements amount to the odd week-end cruise, and a week or so in the summer with the family, will be much attracted by the production line boats with twin bilge-keels and choice of a small inboard motor or a transom fitting to take an outboard. There is a great range of these craft on the market, and while none of them are in top class with regard to performance, they do score heavily when it comes to comfort and versatility, and the designers have done wonders in combining at least a reasonable performance with the latter.

A very comprehensive reference book which lists craft under the heading of Power, Sail, Price and Builders is 'Boat World' published annually by Business Dictionaries Ltd. at Sell's House, 39 East Street, Epsom, Surrey. It costs 20/- and will enable you to start contacting the builders of boats within the price range you select.

Another extremely good reference book in this respect is 'Bristow's Book of Yachts' which is published annually by Navigator Publishing Ltd, High Street, Old Bursledon, Southampton. It costs 21/— and has the great advantage that splendid photographs of all the craft listed accompany the text. Both books are on sale at the larger newsagents and bookshops.

But you might as well know now that when you first go to sight the craft you think may appeal, you will see another just that little bit larger, just that little bit more comfortable, just that little bit more seaworthy. And just that not-so-little bit more expensive! You get, in boats, what you pay for just as with everything else. It is a difficult choice and you will do well to talk to a lot of owners before taking the plunge.

* * *

Reading about anything, and actually doing the thing, are really in two different worlds. One is in the world of the mind where everything that happens is thought out beforehand; the other is in the world of the elements which have a mind of their own and let you know it!

The first few times you go out there in your dinghy all this theory will dissolve in a crystal shower while the elements have a good laugh, but after a few hours Zephyr and Poseidon will prove to be not such bad fellows, and provided you—a mere mortal—are prepared to respect them, they will make staunch allies in a new world of pleasure.

In sailing you do not make your own rules you play the game by theirs! That's the fun of it.

If this book has helped to make those rules more understandable it has achieved its object.

Good sailing!

Index

176